PRAISE FOR *THE SCIENCE OF CUSTOMER CONNECTIONS*

"Fresh, on-point, authentic. Crafting the story that encapsulates your business's value and managing the way that message is shared every day can amplify your volume and extend your reach. Jim Karrh offers a fresh look at messaging, backed by research and years of experience, and provides the tools and playbook template that can help your organization's distinctive voice resonate rather than being lost in background noise. Stop sounding like everyone else and start growing."

—**Whitney Johnson**, LinkedIn 2018 Top Influencer, bestselling author of *Build an A Team* and *Disrupt Yourself*

"In *Relationship Economics*, I wrote that great business relationships are predicated by great conversations. Great conversations come from a fantastic message that's well positioned, managed, and proactively communicated to engage and influence others—their thinking and call to action. Jim Karrh's book is your roadmap, in his interesting, humorous, and insightful manner, to stand up, stand out, and stand beyond the mundane and elevate your presence and business relationships in business conversations."

—**David Nour**, CEO, The Nour Group, Inc., bestselling author, Marshall Goldsmith MG100 member and adjunct faculty at the Goizueta Business School at Emory University

"The volume of information we receive every day is staggering! It's not easy to separate the mindless messages from the mindful ones. Jim's book helps you break free from the message maelstrom and win your audience's hearts and minds."

—**Lisa Nirell**, author of *Energize Growth NOW* and *The Mindful Marketer*, CMO success expert, and founder of Energize-Growth LLC

"With this book, Jim Karrh has taken a lifetime of experience and exploration into the art and science of connecting purposefully, yet meaningfully. Jim has compiled an organized, accessible success guide for smart professionals everywhere. Given that Jim is a man of intelligence and thoughtfulness—someone who walks his talk and knows how to create great conversation experiences—this book is a must-read for those who want to learn how to align their everyday exchanges with the vision and values of their businesses."

—**Patti DeNucci**, author of *The Intentional Networker*

"Jim Karrh's book can unquestionably improve your success. In today's noisy business environment, your ability to influence clients, teammates, executives, leadership, and boards through agile conversations and communication is a 'must have.' Personally, I have witnessed hundreds of technically talented and skilled people neutralize and negate their career potential due to subpar and/or average messaging approaches. I have also seen other, similarly talented individuals who managed to develop and leverage impactful messaging skills; those people performed better, achieved more, and advanced their careers faster. It is an absolute truth: connecting with others through powerful conversations is key to improved performance and relationship building. This book is a must-read for anyone who aspires."

—**Gary Peacock**, retired Chairman, President, and CEO of SunTrust Bank South Division

"I have coached thousands of professionals in the very competitive world of commercial real estate. One of the keys to success is to build a message that attracts and resonates with ideal clients—and to do so consistently. Those of us who offer high-value products and services can't afford to be seen as a commodity! Jim's approach will help you to earn your true value by standing out in everyday business conversations."

—**Rod Santomassimo**, founder of The Massimo Group and author of *Brokers Who Dominate* and *Teams Built to Dominate*

"You really need to read Jim Karrh's book. Every chapter is filled with ideas and examples that will help you be more successful. I read more than one hundred business books a year and would consider this one of the most valuable books I have read in a very long time."

—**John Spence**, leadership and business consultant, coach and author, named by the American Management Association as one of America's Top 50 Leaders to Watch

"Words matter and influence the effectiveness of messaging. The right words sharpen and improve messaging—amplifying its power in a sea of sound bite noise. Jim Karrh's timely, humorous, and intelligent book is must reading for leaders trying to distinguish their voice and rise above competitors in communicating efficiently and with impact!"

—**Toby Hoden**, chief marketing officer for several global investment management firms

the SCIENCE of CUSTOMER CONNECTIONS

Manage Your Message to Grow Your Business

JIM KARRH, PhD

Foreword by Dorie Clark

CAREER PRESS

This edition first published in 2019 by Career Press, an imprint of
Red Wheel/Weiser, LLC
With offices at:
65 Parker Street, Suite 7
Newburyport, MA 01950
www.careerpress.com
www.redwheelweiser.com

ISBN: 978-1-63265-153-2

Library of Congress Cataloging-in-Publication Data available upon
request.

Cover design by Ellen Varitimos
Interior by Maureen Forys, Happenstance Type-O-Rama
Typeset in Warnock Pro, RB No 2.1, and Myriad Pro

Printed in Canada
MAR

10 9 8 7 6 5 4 3 2 1

CONTENTS

PART Three: A New Set of Management Habits

ACKNOWLEDGMENTS

THIS COULD GET DICEY.

Several of my friends who also happen to be authors say this section is one of the toughest to write. There are so many people deserving of thanks and recognition! I will keep this brief, understanding that I will likely commit errors of omission. I apologize in advance.

Being a teacher at heart, I realize how blessed I have been to have had great teachers along the way. At the University of Florida and Duke University's Fuqua School of Business, I learned important concepts from incredibly bright people dedicated to sharing their knowledge. I have continued to learn as I have stayed connected to these two fine institutions.

As a professor myself, I had terrific colleagues at Ithaca College, the University of Alabama, and the University of Arkansas at Little Rock. I learned a lot from my students, too.

I offer my thanks to private-sector employers and work colleagues over the years at Bankers Trust Company, Mountain Valley Spring Company, Mangan Holcomb Partners, and Advantage Communications. My friend Steve Layne had the (probably misguided) courage to go into the tiny-market radio business with me years ago. We never built that media empire, but it was a great experience nonetheless.

For nearly a decade (and counting), I have been a consulting principal with DSG Consulting. It is a privilege to work alongside outstanding consultants in a culture that supports human beings as a whole, with the opportunity to work for clients across industries and around the world.

Coaches also need coaches, and I have had some of the best in the world in Dorie Clark, David Nour, and Alan Weiss.

I am also grateful to those at Arkansas Business Publishing Group, the American Marketing Association, and many other journalists and podcasters who have allowed me to share my ideas with hundreds of thousands of working professionals.

Of course, my clients for consulting and speaking are the best professional source for inspiration and new ideas.

The journey of conceiving, pitching, and writing a book is not for the rational or faint-hearted. My literary agent, John Willig, has guided me through this strange new world with wisdom and warmth.

My family is, in my biased opinion, the best. My profound thanks go to my brother Bill and my in-laws (I have good ones!) for their support. My sons, Miller, Coleman, and Wilson, and my daughter, are the reasons I work hard.

And then there is my wonderful wife Alison. You know what I say about her? She is the best person I know. That's true. I couldn't manage to do anything worthwhile without her.

FOREWORD

IF YOU WANT TO PROSPER, then it's vital for you to stand out and for your voice to be heard. That is increasingly difficult in a noisy business world filled with distractions and disruptions. To make matters worse, much of the conversation gets dragged down by the banal, self-serving, and misleading. How can a talented business professional rise above the noise? How can your valuable and honest message find its way, to be delivered consistently over time by an increasing number of voices?

This is the fundamental issue behind Jim Karrh's work and this book. It has likewise been a common frustration for the hundreds of entrepreneurs, experts, and business leaders whose work I have studied. The fact is, doing your work and talking about it effectively tend to involve different skill sets.

As business professionals, we know our own motivations, plans, and value proposition. We understand our vision and how we differ from our competitors. But our prospective customers—and sometimes even colleagues and employees—might not know the full story. We have to find an effective way to tell our story so that it can be heard and understood by those around us. The businesspeople who have stood out and made the greatest impact decided to be the masters of their own stories and to think a few chess moves ahead.

Any advice to simply keep your head down and work hard is outdated. The nature of work has fundamentally changed. The communication environment is noisier and more fractured. Consumers' expectations continue to rise. New technologies disrupt industry after industry. With more competition from around the globe, there will always be someone who will offer to do your type of work cheaper.

My background includes work as a reporter, political campaign spokesperson, nonprofit executive director, and documentary filmmaker. When I began a solo strategy consulting business, I understood that I would need to take control of my professional life. I needed to establish credibility, to be perceived as someone who was among the best in my field. I would also need a robust network of people who understood what I did. Finally, I would need patience and consistency in my approach. To a large degree, that personal growth strategy mirrored Jim's focus on one's message, messengers, and management habits (although we had not met at the time).

Jim and I first met each other through mutual friends at Duke University's Fuqua School of Business, where I am an adjunct professor and Jim is an alumnus and ambassador. I quickly became interested in Jim's varied experiences as a small-business owner, researcher and university professor, corporate marketing leader, and consultant. You will appreciate the way those experiences have built and sharpened his perspective. His guidance to clients and audiences is both scientifically sound and immediately practical. Jim maintains his teacher's heart. His goal is for you, your organization, and the people you serve to benefit from what he has learned.

Although I have had a measure of success as a consultant, speaker, and author, I'm no extrovert. I've never had formal education in sales or marketing. Yet as you will see in this book, you can manage your message quite well no matter your personality type or level of professional training.

I encourage you to spend some time with Jim's book. Use it to set your messaging priorities, develop ideas, and build consistency in your professional voice. That way, you, with the help of your network of messengers, can make the biggest possible impact.

—DORIE CLARK, author of *Reinventing You, Stand Out,* and *Entrepreneurial You*

INTRODUCTION

WHAT IS THE BEST WAY to talk about your business?

I have been working on the answer to that question for years, mostly for the benefit of clients. I have also tried to figure it out for my own business, especially as the nature of my work has changed dramatically a few times over those years.

Whatever the nature of your business, the conversation matters. It's probably the simplest, most direct way to stand out in our increasingly noisy world. It also represents the fastest way to grow. The social media and online worlds get most of the attention, but the vast majority of word of mouth happens offline. That is where the growth opportunities are hanging out, just waiting.

Too often we miss out. People know us and our organization, but they don't fully understand what we do or whom we serve. Customers and friends would recommend us but aren't sure what to say. The real value we offer is trapped inside industry lingo, technical specifications, and self-focused language.

I am not immune. Not long ago, at some sort of reception, a longtime acquaintance came over to catch up. "Are you still teaching?" he asked. Understand that I was a university professor for several years, although I left the academy fourteen years and two career changes ago. I was surprised by the question but should not have been. It wasn't his fault. In fact, he was both kind enough and interested enough in me to ask a specific question (rather than some bland "How are things?") and drew upon his most recent and accessible memory of my work. It was a reminder to this messaging expert to stay on top of my message.

No one's business is standing still these days. But I have seen very little practical help for professionals or organizational leaders to take advantage of the immense opportunities in front of them. Hence this book.

If managing your message is so important, then why isn't there more guidance? If you scan a typical university course catalog, you'll find no shortage of "management" courses in disciplines such as finance, operations, marketing, or human resources but nothing specific to messaging. If you search online resources for "message management," then you will likely see a lot of content pertaining to tactical areas such as call centers or phone systems. There is clearly a gap. I have a few ideas on why this has been the case.

The first is that message management seems to fall in kind of a mysterious gray zone or intersection among areas such as sales, marketing, customer service, and interpersonal communication. Inside larger enterprises, it's easy to find people with "manager" in their title, but I have yet to find anyone who has Message Manager on his or her business card. It is difficult to know who should be in charge of the everyday conversations of the business, even though those conversations are vitally important to the business.

I believe there are a couple of other important psychological forces at work here as well. One is that the mere idea of "managing" organic everyday conversations in a business might seem like a fool's chase, inherently unmanageable.

"People are going to say what they're going to say, aren't they?" asked a skeptical executive. The practical realities that I have found, however, are much more encouraging. Managing the everyday message of an organization is just as plausible, practical, and profitable as managing a financial portfolio, a plant operation, or a compliance process. There are implications for growing revenue, building efficiency, and lowering exposure.

Managing your message is about clarifying your value to others and motivating human behavior, which itself has great consequences for the organization. This book is designed to make things simple and accessible.

There is one other sticking point that I have seen. Some professionals might acknowledge the importance of a consistent and effective message, and even buy into the idea that the process might actually be manageable—for someone else. They worry that because they aren't messaging experts or extroverts or creatives or great conversationalists themselves, they are ill-suited to be a messaging leader for their organization. In other words, they might say, "Jim, an MBA or a CPA could make for a good chief financial officer or financial manager. It probably takes an engineer or a process expert to be an operations manager. Who am I to manage my message or anyone else's? I can't even describe to my mother what I do for a living." Well, have I got a book for you!

I wrote *The Science of Customer Connections* with a certain set of business professionals in mind, the sort that I have had the privilege of working alongside over the years. Some are just starting out. Some are making profound changes in their career. Some are well along a professional track. Some are in business largely for themselves as agents, franchisees, independent contractors, or solo-preneurs. Some work for big corporations, others for professional associations or nonprofits. They work in fields from the technical to the creative, be that in IT, healthcare, technology, logistics, materials handling, financial services, insurance, or even the martial arts. But they share certain things.

Their business depends, in large part, on the spoken word—the everyday conversations that affect their business and its future. They often struggle to find their own way to talk about their business, and they might doubt their ability to lead a process or inspire others to do the same. They're busy. They have lots of priorities competing for their attention. And they are acutely aware that any initiatives for the business had better not create a bunch of busy work.

This book combines some simple principles that I have learned over the years, a lot of useful research, and the experiences of others into frameworks that you can follow. As you apply them, your business will grow—without you necessarily having to change your business model or elements such as your offerings, pricing, or distribution. In my experience, the process will produce a renewed sense of energy and clarity about your business and an enthusiasm for spreading the word.

I encourage you to read this book with a purpose. Consider the questions at the end of chapters and find ways to get started that make the most sense for you, your team, and your priorities for growth. Take your time, but don't let the concepts remain in the conceptual. As you begin to apply these principles and tips, you will gain skill and confidence. You don't need to be a PhD, an MBA, a researcher, a creative professional, an extrovert, or anything else to build new growth opportunities for your business, your idea, or your cause.

Welcome to the game, Message Manager.

Let's work to make sure your business story is shared well, and often.

1

YOUR MESSAGE CAN BE YOUR BUSINESS ADVANTAGE—
If It Isn't Hiding Somewhere

EVERY BUSINESS PROFESSIONAL, and every organization, has a message worth sharing. After all, if we didn't have something valuable to say and offer, then what would be the point of the business?

Your business also needs to grow—whether that growth is measured in revenue, profit, opportunities for increasingly interesting work, or deeper engagement with customers and communities (or all of the above!). Growth, however you define it for your business, is better for everyone. Rising revenue and profit means more financial reward as well as fuel for investing in the future of the business. Building more options and opportunities means you can work on the products and projects that you want (and shed those that are a drag or distraction). Customers, clients, and members appreciate their relationship with you even more because they like dealing with others who are successful.

Growth is also necessary. The alternative is decline and decay; no team or organization can just stand pat or decide to catch its collective breath for a few years. Competition and disruption in the marketplace simply won't allow that to happen.

As important as growth might be, it isn't easy to come by. Many leadership teams focus on major strategic moves such as new product or service lines, locations, technology investments, acquisitions, or partnerships. Any or all of those might be a consideration for your business. But while you and your team evaluate those sorts of big bets, know that there is also one big growth opportunity that tends to be overlooked: how the very people who are closest to your business talk about the business every day.

As Jonah Berger noted in his book *Contagious: Why Things Catch On*, only 7 percent of word of mouth happens online. That's right—despite all of the attention we pay to social media, there is thirteen times more word-of-mouth activity in the offline world. I would never suggest that the online side of things is not important for your organization. But the numbers are clear, and it isn't even close. If your organization is looking for above-average growth, then why not set your priorities squarely on the area with thirteen times more opportunity?

If that statistic surprises you—and it does surprise many businesspeople—then consider this very reasonable explanation. Online conversations are easy to see (and record, or even search). Our offline conversations, by contrast, tend to go unnoticed. We chat in hallways, at sporting events, on neighborhood walks, and in innumerable other settings. Those everyday messages might be invisible, but they are impactful on what we believe and how we act. And they are, to a large degree, manageable. By knowing where to look, and by following some simple habits, you and your team can lead a consistent competency that in turn puts you in the middle of those extra growth opportunities.

Across dozens of organizations—large and small, corporate and nonprofit, across industries—I have seen how improving everyday business messaging can both grow the business and improve the engagement of all the people in it. You don't necessarily need to change your products, prices, distribution strategy, geographic reach, organizational chart, or the people themselves.

I have heard executives variously describe this as "the secret sauce," "the missing bullet," and "the missing piece we didn't realize was missing." I have come to recognize it as a potential growth engine that is hiding in plain sight.

The great news is that effective business messaging isn't all that mysterious in practice. It does, however, require the leadership to become very intentional about (1) everyone's understanding of the most important "must-knows," (2) building base skills for leading customer conversations, and (3) socializing and managing the effort in a way that everyone becomes confident in his or her role. That's why a plan and playbook are so helpful in building success. By the way, if you're a leader or solo professional, then you might also need to shed some widely held but false and damaging assumptions along the way.

While advising many very competent and hard-working business professionals over the years, I have found that many get uptight when it comes to their messaging. They don't know quite how to approach it. They are excited about their actual work, yet in the everyday opportunities for them and their teams to talk about the work they find frustration and misses. Some have tried leaving this whole messaging thing to their marketing departments or an outside agency to figure out—and report that the essence of what they want to say gets lost in the creative fog of slogans, taglines, and advertising copy. Others have let the sales or development teams run with the message in a whatever-sells approach—which led to as many different messages as there were messengers. Some leaders have taken the messaging burden on themselves alone, believing they are the only one who really "gets it" well enough to share it.

None of those approaches can fully scale your business for growth. Lack of clarity means you will likely lose lots of deals and potential relationships (and lose pricing power in the deals you do win). Inconsistency erodes your brand and reputation. And no business will prosper over the long haul with a frustrated, burned-out leader and a core message that is stuck in the office.

This very day, there are probably competitors whose offerings aren't any better (or maybe not even as good) as yours but who are grabbing more opportunities simply by virtue of having more and better conversations. That's not right. It does not have to persist.

Your path to far more effective everyday business messaging is right there to follow. Neither you nor your colleagues have to be trained communicators, brilliant conversationalists, extraverts, or "slimy sales-y" (as one client described what she wanted to avoid). Nor do business leaders have to be some sort of messaging hero in a cape, unless of course that's their wardrobe thing. You can create growth opportunities through a simple, practical approach, taking into account all of the noise in the marketplace as well as the inherent anxieties, limitations, and unrecognized strengths of the people around your business. Furthermore, your efforts need not be perfect. Just by being intentional and consistent about the everyday message, your business will be establishing an important, long-term advantage.

You will need a plan. By a "plan," I do not mean a dense strategy document, a bunch of statistical research, or a flowery creative guide. Rather, your plan will be based on the best things that people are already doing today as they talk about the business with other people. It will synthesize all of the things you and your colleagues could say (which is probably overwhelming) into a few conversational nuggets that real human beings can remember and use when the moment is right. It will be based on sound research into business messaging and what makes it tick.

You'll want to get started. It's not like the world is going to be less noisy anytime soon.

THE MESSAGING WORLD IS TURNING FASTER

We can agree that there is no shortage of communication activity in our markets. Of course, people have always had a proclivity to talk. In the past, the settings were more likely to be hallways, street corners, club meetings, church social halls, barbershops, salons, and a non-mobile phone. (My mother had a certain chair where she would sit, usually with a cup of coffee nearby, for phone conversations with friends.)

The explosive growth of social and digital media has smashed most of those previous limitations of accessibility, location, and time constraints. Today, the practice of sharing and consuming messages takes ever-larger chunks of most people's time. Social media, as the primary example, has crowded out other foundational elements of everyday life. How much so? The marketing agency Mediakix added together the average time spent each day on YouTube, Facebook, Snapchat, Instagram, and Twitter, and then projected the total over a typical young adult's lifetime. They concluded that an average person will spend more than five years of their lives on social media! That total still trails the time spent watching television but came in well ahead of the total time those same people will spend on eating/ drinking, grooming, socializing, or the necessary evil of doing laundry. Insert your favorite joke here about the people who live on social media not smelling very good.

Our attention spans are shorter than ever as well. This long-term trend has only accelerated in recent years, and message creators of all stripes are trying to keep up. As just one example, a research team led by Cornell University psychologist James E. Cutting found that from 1935 to the modern day movies have progressively used shorter scenes, more motion and movement, and darker settings. The research team concluded, "We believe that all of them have been created by filmmakers seeking to control the attention of their viewers, and possibly to enhance viewer involvement in film." Now filmmakers even have to deal with audiences who are using their mobile devices and social media during the movie. (Have you been to a theater lately?)

Back in high school, I needed money to help pay for a car and gas; I found a job in my small hometown as a deejay for a country-music radio station. I learned a radio term that applies very well to our digital communication environment today. The "signal-to-noise ratio" compares the level of the signal you desire to send (such as, in that case, a Willie Nelson song) to the level of background noise (such as static). The higher that ratio, the better. Today, the opportunity for "noise" to mess with your intended signal is greater than ever. The noise in your messaging system is in part due to the ways that those technological leaps in communication are absorbing the hours in our days. It's also a function of our more limited attention spans and propensity for distraction. One of today's country-music stars, Kenny Chesney, had a big hit with his song "Noise."

So this is the increasingly noisy conversational world where our businesses reside. We can't get away from it. The smart strategy would seem to involve something other than just shouting louder—to instead get our message into more of the natural, common conversations where noise levels are less imposing and audiences might pay attention.

But what about your team's capacity to talk about the business effectively in those settings . . . in other words, what can your quality of signal be?

MESSENGERS AND MANAGERS ARE CHANGING, AND NOT ALWAYS FOR THE BETTER

Most people have a natural inclination to seek, process, and share information. The massive demand for social media and wireless communication services provides plenty of evidence for that. Yet the level of communication skills that people have (or rather, lack) today is posing a big challenge to employers.

I hear a lot of complaints from executives and team leaders about the lack of communication and conversational skills in their organizations. They see problems popping up in many important settings: job applications full of errors, interviews in which candidates can't convey a clear thought, reports or emails that expose writing problems, and employees' seeming unwillingness to talk to colleagues or customers face to face. "We have trouble," an HR leader told me. "This wave of new workers seems most comfortable talking with their thumbs." (She was demonstrating a texting motion on an imaginary smartphone while saying this.) This isn't good for those businesspeople or the business overall.

Younger workers get much of the criticism. Although some of that might be natural generational friction, it's also true that Millennials show an abrupt break from their predecessors when it comes to communication. (By the way, my view is that categories such as "Millennials" are often used too broadly but because a lot of research into younger workers was defined that way, I have to report it as such in order to be consistent. I trust you'll recognize the larger point.) A Bank of America study found that, on an average day, 39 percent of Millennials interact with their smartphone more than with anything or anyone else; that compares to 29 percent of other Americans (still not necessarily good). Our devices are a common way to avoid other social interactions, too; more than 70 percent of Millennials admit to doing that, compared to 44 percent of other Americans. This does not necessarily portend the end of Western civilization, but as you'll see detailed in later chapters it does require an approach to messaging that takes new realities of engagement into account. Leaders need to prepare their younger workers to coach and lead others, and quickly. Those who simply moan about "kids these days," like Granddad on his porch, won't be able to adapt.

Business leaders need to find their best combination of improved signal and lower noise in the middle of this new communication environment. Organizations themselves are learning to play in a more mobile, digital world. But individual business professionals also need to communicate and work effectively across age groups, personalities, locations, and cultures. This tension begs a couple of questions: Can we simplify and clarify our understanding of business messaging so that a leader can know where and how to address it in his or her organization? And can we present information in a way so that diverse work teams can harness more messaging opportunities?

BUSINESS MESSAGING SITS ON A THREE-LEGGED STOOL

Some businesses seem to have figured this out better than most. Their customers or clients tend to be not just satisfied but actual raving fans, proudly and frequently sharing their experiences with friends. The employees have a clear sense of exactly what the company does, whom it serves, and for what benefit; their clarity in turn becomes an organic, gravitational pull for recruiting new employees. The vendors, alumni, and other friends of the business likewise are pretty much on the same page. A powerful growth engine is at work. The question for other businesses is: how do I get some of that?

I have had the same curiosity. Fortunately, I have been able to examine many different types of organizations over many years and through different lenses. As a PhD and consumer researcher, I have had access to the big picture of persuasion and behavior. As a corporate marketing leader, I had to get very practical in changing our message and how it was conveyed; although we were far from perfect, in just two years our little niche brand was judged to have the best integrated marketing and public relations program in the huge global bottled-water industry. These days, as a consultant and speaker, I work with leaders to help them implement new messages as part of their growth strategies. These experiences have revealed to me a rather simple yet powerful model for understanding how to go on offense with business messaging.

This model has three components. The degree to which they fit and work together determine whether your business messaging will either help you grow or hold you back:

- **The Message.** Your message could potentially encompass dozens and dozens of specifics, ranging from your vision or mission statement to the company's history to its logo to product details. And that's part of the problem in equipping people with a message for everyday use. For our purposes, we will focus on carving out simple, conversational language with a healthy dollop of storytelling; those are the messages people tend to remember and share in customer conversations. Save the other stuff for the website (or leave it out of there, too).

- **The Messengers.** These are the people with whom you want to share the message, on the job and in the community. Your portfolio of potential messengers is probably larger than you think. Many leaders limit themselves by thinking too narrowly according to job roles (only the sales or service people) and personalities (only the extroverts). We'll cast a wider net, make it easy for the messengers, and help everyone avoid big potential mistakes.

- **Management Habits.** The organizations that excel at messaging don't think of this as some time-limited promotional campaign. Instead, their leaders made a conscious decision to change for the long term how everyone in the business would talk about the business. They keep things fresh, model the right behaviors, coach their direct reports, and establish a few simple habits and reminders.

Now think of those components as the legs of a three-legged stool. We need the three legs to be of equal length and strength for the stool to be a strong foundation. (The other chapters of this book are divided among message, messengers, and management.)

If your business is small, then the legs of the stool might be short but the overall structure strong. When I was chief marketing officer of that bottled-water company, it was easier to keep those components aligned than it would have been for one of the industry giants. If you're managing a big team or organization—and the legs of the stool get longer—things can get wobbly in a hurry. Just as a carpenter would see the need to add some well-engineered bracing to the legs, managers in growing organizations have to build systems of internal communication, training, and onboarding.

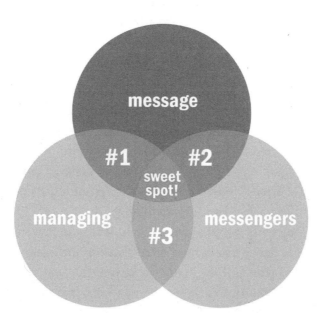

WHEN IT GOES WRONG: CRICKETS, COWBOYS, AND COMMODITIES

If business messaging really does sit on a three-legged foundation, then we need to make sure each of the legs is strong enough to hold up under pressure. Often they don't. When one leg is weak compared to the other two, then the structure will collapse in the direction of the weakness—with predictable, painful results.

How would you know if you have a particular point of weakness? Well, consider these three comments—all paraphrasing things I have heard lots of times from business leaders:

- "There just isn't any buzz about our business."

- "We can't seem to stay on message."

- "We have a strong value proposition, but that doesn't get across."

Each represents weakness in a different leg. On several occasions I have had to learn (the hard way) about these weaknesses and how best to address them. Do any of these ring true in your business?

- **Crickets: Too few people are using the message.** During the summer evenings in my small Georgia hometown, you could usually hear lots of crickets chirping. That was because there were no other sounds; not much was happening! Today, "crickets chirping" is a popular phrase to point out silence, as when a bad joke is followed by . . . um, not much of anything from the audience. In business, a similar lack of buzz or response is the enemy of growth. If this is your symptom, the underlying cause probably involves your messengers (as in not having enough of them). This is Gap #1 in the Message Management Model.

Years after my high school deejay-ing experience, I was co-owner of two tiny-market radio stations. As is often the case with a small-business operation, the owner (yours truly) did a little of everything. My business partner and I were even the morning-show hosts. It was fun—for a while—but we put too much on our own shoulders. We needed help. I see a similar weight on other entrepreneurs and small-business leaders. If you're in that boat, I ask: Are you equipping and encouraging enough people to take the message to their networks of peers and friends?

- **Cowboys: Everyone is doing it their way.** Does it seem like everyone in the business tells their own story in their own way? If people are "rolling their own" (as one client described it) and delivering messages inconsistently, then you have a management issue. This is Gap #2, and it can be fixed.

Corporate marketing leaders often have the role of "brand cop" (as my former CEO called me), assigned control of the marketing assets and standards of the organization. They take that role seriously. If team members in the field are telling different stories and making inconsistent claims, then over time potential customers won't know what or whom to trust. One marketing leader complained that one week after a carefully prepared and vetted PowerPoint was distributed to the sales team, there were already eight different modified versions making the rounds. On the other hand, teams that are generally consistent in their messaging—even allowing a little wiggle room for people to express a bit of autonomy—build credibility. Is there enough consistency in how your message is delivered across teams and roles?

- **Commodities: We sound like everyone else.** Some businesses have unintentionally allowed their messages to become bland, boring, and self-centered. They speak in acronyms and industry lingo. They convey a lot more about their passion and great intentions than about the value they bring to customers. This is Gap #3.

One of the biggest red flags I see is when a business leader says something like, "We need to educate the market." I was once an educator myself, teaching at three universities and publishing research in a bunch of journals (that probably dozens of people read). Professor types are the quintessential subject-matter experts, whose audience of students basically shows up because they have to. Let's not fall into the trap of trying to educate the market but instead aim to engage it. Sometimes a seemingly simple change in language or tone can make a huge difference. Are the words, phrases, and stories of your business separating you from the pack?

A PLAYBOOK APPROACH WORKS

There is a simple, proven approach for getting past chirping crickets, commoditization, and cowboy behavior—one that builds consistency in customer conversations across the organization without some overbearing script or massive education process. The answer is a "playbook," a concept that has grown in use far beyond sports teams to include many work teams and entire companies. No clipboards, whistles, or embarrassing shorts required! Organizations use playbooks quite successfully for a variety of purposes. For business messaging, playbooks include bite-sized talking points with guidance on how to engage customers, share stories, and convey the things that make an organization unique. A properly constructed playbook matches the learning and conversational styles of attention-starved workers.

Unfortunately, some leaders get enamored with the idea of a playbook but don't fully understand how to create one or coach to it. This book will guide you through the process, step by step, in a way that you can tailor to your business needs.

I recommend that you and your team begin with a clear understanding of what a good playbook is and is not:

- **Good playbooks are *not* rule books.** Playbooks don't take the place of employee manuals or handbooks, nor should they read like a legal document or car owner's manual. We know how everyone feels about those documents, right? They are created to be comprehensive, covering every conceivable circumstance and generally protecting the corporate rear end. For our purposes, we will go for simple over complex and less over more.

- **Good playbooks are *not* libraries of product descriptions or sales collateral.** Messaging playbooks—if used properly—are great for helping the business grow. Some bosses, frustrated at disconnects between sales and marketing, try to force the issue. They might create a library or repository for all of their sales collateral, toss in the content, call the finished product a playbook, and nag the sales team to use it. That approach does help everyone to know where to locate things, but it provides no guidance on when and how to use the information.

- **Good playbooks *are* guides for specific conversations.** In team sports, coaches use playbooks so that all team members know exactly what to do in specific plays—which themselves are designed for specific goals (e.g., score quickly, convert a third down, or run time off the game clock). For business messaging, we organize playbook content around certain conversations, audiences, or initiatives—omitting stale, irrelevant, or overly complicated content. That strategy helps everyone stay focused and move faster.

When a journalist in Maine asked a group of successful high school football coaches about playbooks and how they used them, he found some variations. A few coaches still use actual books with hand-stenciled routes and formations. Others have adopted digital versions so that players and coaches can see all of the content on their phones. But there was unanimity on one point: keep it simple. "It can turn into a monster real quick," one coach said. "You can get carried away and try to get cute and creative." The value of the playbook approach lies not in the playbook itself, but rather in the behaviors and opportunities that happen because of it.

Let's Start Building Your Plan

Just as coaches select specific plays in support of an overall strategy or game plan, you will want to get clear on the business purpose of the playbook, including the specific behaviors and business outcomes that the playbook should help produce. (Along the way, the people you expect to use the playbook will ask themselves or you, "So why are we doing this?") It's also a good practice to involve all of the relevant business units or functions as you create and validate your playbook content. That might include high performers from sales, marketing, product development, operations, or finance. You might also involve some great customers who will provide honest feedback.

Remember that your playbook is not an exercise in command and control. Rather, it's about strategy, simplicity, understanding of roles, and the importance of practice and coaching. It will serve as the bracing that keeps your three-legged stool strong as you grow.

The first step in building your playbook is to get clarity on its "why."

TAKE A MANAGER MOMENT . . .

- What specifically is the value of great messaging to you professionally? How about to your organization?
- Think of a progression from what is true today to what is possible and valuable for your business in the near future. I have provided a couple of samples, but of course your mileage will differ . . .

BUSINESS FUNCTION/ACTIVITY	WHERE WE ARE TODAY	WHERE WE COULD BE	VALUE TO THE BUSINESS
Selling more of our product portfolio to existing customers	40% of customers buy more than one thing from us.	Up to 50% in 12 months	20–25% more revenue
Getting our new hires productive, understanding what we do	We train on specific jobs and sometimes on products.	Everyone knows what we offer, why, and the benefits to customers.	Higher employee engagement

Part One

A MESSAGE FOR GROWTH

2

MAKING THE MESSAGE:
What Can We Say?

LET'S IMAGINE THAT IT IS TIME to sell your home. (If, on the other hand, you're ever going to be in the market to buy an existing home, you'll still want to follow along. This story might save you money.) It will be important to use the right language in your listing so that you can generate the greatest possible interest from potential buyers—which should help you position your home to sell at the highest possible price. So what exactly should you say?

You have been cleaning and decluttering the house to make it look great. Friends and neighbors are telling you that the house should sell easily. "It's so inviting," one says. "It's in great shape," says another. "It really is in move-in condition for the right family."

Hmmmm. "Inviting" sounds like a great descriptor to put in the listing. Or should you say it's in "move-in condition" instead? This is not a frivolous decision. Considering the average sales price of existing single-family homes in the United States as of this writing, your choice of one term over the other would likely make a nearly $3,000 difference in the sale price of your home.

SOME WORDS GET USED A LOT

There is no shortage of hyped-up promotional language in business today. Have we not heard enough of "world-class," "new and improved," "epic," "innovate," and "disruptive"? But let's take the long view. As it turns out, a few words have proven popular for many years in the world of marketing and persuasion.

There are several excellent collections of advertising from past decades, including the Advertising Archives (a resource for British and American press advertising) and Duke University's John W. Hartman Center for Sales, Advertising, & Marketing History. If, for whatever reason, you decided to devote several hours to a careful examination of ads from a generation ago—when print and television advertising were dominant—then you would likely notice some consistent patterns in the actual words used. *You* and *your* were popular. So were promotional words such as *more, new, like, taste,* and *first,* plus quality claims such as *better, world, people,* and of course *quality.* But what about the social media platforms of today?

When the social media management service Hootsuite analyzed nearly 40,000 Facebook ads, the most popular word was—you guessed it—*you.* Next in order were *free, now, new, up, more, out, today, find, shop, business, save,* and *time.* Notice that *you, more,* and *new* keep showing up.

I suspect that the differences are due to the immediacy of online and social channels. When print (and broadcast network TV) advertising were dominant, there was a separation in time and place between the seller's message and the consumer's opportunity to buy. Words such as *quality, taste, great, best, better,* and *choice* were well suited to that world. These days, consumers can immediately search, compare, ask, and buy; it shouldn't surprise us that *today*, *shop*, *find*, and *time* have become more popular for sellers.

Nevertheless, the differences pale in comparison to the commonalities. Over several decades, persuasive messages have consistently focused on how you can get more of something good, and the seller is sharing this information as if it were big news. If everyone tends to use a lot of the same words, are there ways to stand out? Can some words work better than others? Let's go back to the home-selling example to answer more definitively.

SOME WORDS WORK A LOT BETTER THAN OTHERS

The world of residential real estate is a great testing ground for the power of words. Every house is a bit different, of course, but they have comparable types of features (square footage, age, architectural style, etc.) that can be described in different and creative ways. Sellers use the words in their listings to attract interest and set expectations, whereas potential buyers use those same words to screen through what's available and often to frame their price negotiations. There are some specific, quantifiable results (selling price, discount or premium to listing price, days on market, etc.) that—given a large enough sample—offer clear evidence of what was genuinely effective and what was less so.

We can guess that certain words and phrases would drag home prices down. You and I can imagine (or remember) instances when verbiage is used in an attempt to cover problems: a "breathtaking" house might have been inhabited by a chain smoker, "cozy" means tiny, and a "peek-a-boo view" puts you at risk of falling off a balcony or pulling a neck muscle to see it!

A research team led by Kimberly Goodwin studied more than 16,000 such transactions, and their listing descriptions, from a nine-year period in an area of Virginia. The team wasn't terribly interested in standard stuff such as the number of bedrooms and bathrooms. Rather, they were investigating the impact of more unique features and language on sales prices and timing. Not surprisingly, the house listings that included specific property characteristics (like granite countertops or wainscoting) sold at a premium and were also 9.2 percent more likely to sell.

Those are features that are part and parcel of the product (house) itself. What was really interesting is, given a set of features, the impact of different words selected to promote houses to buyers and buyers' agents. The researchers found that a few "positive opinion words" moved the needle on actual prices. During the nine-year period under study, each positive opinion word boosted sale prices by an average of 0.9 percent. Some word examples were *inviting, spacious,* and *stunning.* That means just three positive words applied to a $300,000 home's description would translate into an average bump in price of $8,100. Not too shabby, huh?

In a different study, Canadian researcher Paul Anglin found that the word *beautiful* boosted sales price but good value reduced sales prices by 6 percent. Move-in condition had no effect. The phrases *handyman's special* and *rental property* were value killers, reducing sales value by up to 30 percent.

So, if in our example you chose *inviting* over *move-in condition,* then you would likely have pocketed a lot more cash for the exact same house.

That's an impressive use of words to build value in the residential real estate world. How about language that works more broadly, across industry lines? During the course of my years as a consumer researcher, copywriter, and corporate marketer, I have seen a lot of attempts to turn a profitable phrase. A few words have proven effective over time and in different settings. Here is my starter list:

- **You.** Okay, that one was easy. It was the single most popular word in print ads thirty years ago and it is the most popular in Facebook ads these days. And it sure beats *I.*

- **Because.** This word appeals to our logical selves, helping the audience connect the dots and establish cause-and-effect relationships. (However, as a father of three I cannot report that telling your kids "Because I said so" will be effective.)

- **New.** What's new? From fashion trends to the "New & Noteworthy" category of podcasts on iTunes, our attention tends to automatically go to what seems novel or different. That's why reporters talk about the news, right?

- **Most.** This word can be used to establish priorities ("what is most important to you") as well as to offer evidence of social proof, or what is most popular with others ("most people in your situation choose this"). When they're unsure of the best decision, people tend to look to similar others for cues.

- **Options.** Most people (see what I did there?) want a sense of freedom, and push back when they feel trapped. It is best to offer multiple options rather than to force a binary, take-it-or-leave-it approach. I prefer the word *options* over *choices,* because the word *choice* also describes a decision that for some people produces anxiety. A common messaging mistake involves presenting options without appropriate guidance, so get comfortable with this next word . . .

- **Recommend.** A sound and empathetic recommendation is based on both your expertise and your understanding of the audience's situation. Recommending is better than merely suggesting and much better than simply asking, "What do you want to do?" without offering any direction. This isn't about being pushy to close a deal, either. A true professional's recommendation is offered to lead someone to a decision that benefits everyone.

- **Imagine.** I have a confession to make. Although a number of other experts have for years touted this word for its persuasive power, I resisted for a long time. It seemed a bit, well, staged. Could I with a straight face say something like, "Just imagine a world where your story is always understood and appreciated . . . ooh, look, there's a unicorn sliding down that rainbow!" The social-scientist part of me was willing to keep a slightly open mind, however, and I have now come around. There is enough good research for us to conclude that, at least in some cases, the things we imagine can alter the way we see the real world. As one example, a study in the journal *Current Biology* revealed that the process of imagining hearing something can change what we later see. The reverse was also true; what subjects imagined seeing changed what they actually heard later.

I am not recommending that you or your team try to cram these words into every conversation or communication.

Please don't! But they can certainly serve as a useful comparison to the messages you are using today. Are you using powerful words in those precious conversational opportunities?

While you are adding effective words to your repertoire, you might find some others that deserve to be sent packing. Many words carry a little too much baggage, thus provoking skepticism and unease:

- **Sell.** If you tell consumers that you are going to sell them something, then you are setting up a competition ("Oh, really? Well, give it your best shot!"). Nevertheless, sellers such as auto dealers routinely say things like, "We want to sell you your next car." Is it any wonder that more than 80 percent of Americans say they dislike buying at traditional auto dealers and more than 60 percent feel taken advantage of there?

- **Buy.** Buying involves parting with one's hard-earned money, so it represents the negative part of shopping. The more positive part comes in owning, using, and enjoying the stuff we bought. Consider talking about the pleasures of having your product or service rather than the act of paying for it.

- **Contract.** Formal contracts are necessary, but they are tilted toward (and generally provide more emotional comfort to) sellers over buyers. "Agreement" is a friendlier term.

- **Cheap.** Some companies have successfully marketed "cheap flights" or "cheap seats," but that works because consumers know that seats on the same flight are directly comparable. In most cases, however, cheapness is considered a code word for something that is inferior or of poor quality.

Consider how you as a consumer would react to a pitch like this one: "We sell cars cheap! Sign this contract and buy now."

PUT YOUR MISSION STATEMENT ASIDE . . . PLEASE

Your mission statement is probably a poor substitute for a real marketplace message. Most mission statements (or value statements, or vision statements) focus on the organization, its intentions, and its wonderful motivations. These can be pure and true, yet still largely irrelevant to most external audiences most of the time.

Mission statements are almost always developed in big committees. They emerge only after a long, arduous journey through many meetings to make sure everyone's voice is heard. That's fine, but you and I know that committees aren't exactly known as fountainheads of innovation. Even across companies in different industries and markets, mission statements can sound eerily alike.

The Mission Statement Book includes 301 mission statements from some of the top corporations in the United States. The great adman Jeremy Bullmore went through those 301 statements to find the most frequently used words (an act of bravery). If you are into clichés, then you will admire his tally. *Service* was the top word, appearing in 230, or 76 percent, of the statements. The rest of the top ten, in descending order: *customers, quality, value, employees, growth, environment, profit, leader,* and *best.*

There is nothing inherently wrong with those words. But none are particularly engaging or memorable, either. It is far more effective to craft messages that are less about you and more about what your audience can do—with your help, of course.

WHY LESS IS MORE AND SIMPLER IS BETTER

The right words matter, but you can do too much of an otherwise good thing. Businesses and professionals have a shrinking window of time to get attention; when a lot of words appear, many time-pressed people turn away. In that Virginia real estate study, researchers found that more words in a listing led to less likelihood of a sale. Plus, if there was a sale, lengthy narratives wound up reducing the ultimate sale price by 6 percent.

Okay, so we'll zip it. But what about the quality of words, not just the volume of them? How simple or complex should your message be?

In his portrayal of an attorney in the movie Philadelphia, Denzel Washington spoke this line to a prospective client: "Explain this to me like I'm a six-year-old, okay?" That is a vivid (and a bit depressing) instance of dumbing things down. But as it turns out, in some messaging scenarios Mr. Washington's character doesn't miss the mark by much. A team from Boomerang for Gmail examined a collection of more than 40 million business emails. Their study showed that emails written at a third-grade reading level had the highest response rate. Those emails had 17 percent higher response rates than emails written at a high school reading level and 36 percent higher open rates than those written at a college reading level.

Let's not immediately start emailing customers and prospects like they're eight-year-olds. The value you offer and the actions you recommend are well beyond a third-grader's understanding. But even in high-value business conversations, simple language tends to win. These days, a more informal and conversational style tends to be most effective. That doesn't mean coming across as juvenile but rather, respecting our audiences enough to make it simple for them.

THERE'S A COMMON NOISE COMING FROM YOUR INDUSTRY

When it comes to messaging, your industry might be working against you. That isn't intentional on anyone's part; industry groups and meetings are great vehicles for sharing good practices, forming policy, and establishing relationships. When I speak to industry associations, it is clear to me that these professional tribes can be very beneficial to everyone involved.

The sticky issue is that, over time, people within any given group or tribe can tend to start acting and sounding the same. Think of a messaging undertow that drags a lot of people downward and closer together.

It's true that professionals are changing jobs and organizations more frequently. Oftentimes, however, they change jobs within the same industry. Government, aerospace/defense, media, telecommunications, nonprofits, restaurants, and healthcare are examples of industries where workers tend to stay, even as they change roles and employers.

What happens when people stay within the same general tribe year after year? They attend the same conferences, adopt similar insider language, and share similar stories. Think back to our concept of the signal-to-noise ratio; many industries unwittingly and unknowingly perpetuate a layer of messaging noise across the membership.

Here is a vivid and timely example. The next time you're going through a magazine or scanning signs at a sporting event or airport, take a moment to notice the ads for watches. More than 90 percent of today's ads for watches show the time as 10:10, or something very close to it. That is not a coincidence.

It was very different during the 1930s and 1940s, when many of the ads for clocks and pocket watches showed the time as 8:20. That meant a nice symmetry for the placement of the hands—our brains like symmetry—and also left space for the reader to easily see the brand name or logo (which is typically centered near the top of the face). What changed?

By the late 1950s, a failing market researcher named James Vicary was making news. He claimed that, by flashing the messages "Eat Popcorn" and "Drink Coca-Cola" for just fractions of a second during movie previews, he could increase sales for theater owners. A few years later it became clear Vicary had faked the study. Nevertheless, there was growing public awareness and concern about the power of subliminal advertising.

If you think of a clock or watch face as akin to a human face, then the 8:20 position of the hands could—supposedly in some subliminal way—look like a frown. The 10:10 position, just as symmetrical, could look like a smile. And wouldn't a subliminal smile produce more sales than a nasty subliminal frown?

Over time, we have learned that claims about subliminal advertising are so much rubbish. There is zero evidence that any of that stuff makes any real-world difference in consumer behavior. (If it did, it would be the worst-kept secret in marketing history!) Nevertheless, an industry's 10:10 practice that started more than half a century ago is still going strong. Many of the industry's leaders have even institutionalized it; Timex policy dictates that timepieces (even the digital ones) are set to exactly 10:09:36, while at Rolex watches are always photographed at 10:10:31.

It gets even more strange and entrenched. Reporters found that industry leaders recognize the practice but have little idea why it exists. Not long ago, I was visiting with a local Rolex dealer inside his store. He is both knowledgeable and successful, yet he had no idea why the large Rolex poster on his wall—like every other Rolex ad out there—showed a watch set to 10:10. That is how industry thinking works. Smart and well-intentioned people get sucked into following convention with little or no idea why they are doing so.

As you develop the words and phrases to describe your business, don't just default to the assumptions, language, or images that have been common in your industry. Those assumptions may no longer be valid. And why would you necessarily want to say things the way everyone else has been saying them for years? The world of watch advertising might be the only place where time actually stands still.

THE VALUE OF AUTHENTICITY, OR WHY TRUTH AND TRADITION AREN'T THE SAME

Authenticity is a popular buzzword, but in my experience it is less of a fad than a practical return to a proven messaging practice. Consumers want organizations of all types to be more "real." Few of us want to be seen as phonies, and that extends to the products and services we use.

This can be tricky for organizations. Who doesn't want to put their best foot forward? How much should they reveal? I have found that when organizations fail to be authentic, they aren't necessarily trying to pull a fast one in their marketplace. Rather, they confuse authenticity with tradition, long-standing habits, or their good intentions. In some cases, companies can hurt themselves by being unconsciously inauthentic.

In 2004, I came from outside the bottled-water industry to lead marketing for the Mountain Valley Spring Company. Our signature product was a single-source natural spring water, bottled in both glass and recyclable plastic at a protected watershed near Hot Springs, Arkansas. The bottled-water industry was (and still is) dominated by huge companies such as Nestlé, Pepsico, and the Coca-Cola Company; their offerings include waters blended from multiple springs or purified from municipal sources. Our little company was different in that our signature brand came from one spring.

Despite this high-quality product, the company's sales had been stagnant for years. We needed to make some changes. I quickly targeted a product label that featured a drawing of three snow-capped mountains with a river running among them. I made my case at a management meeting. The discussion went something like this:

Me: *"This label is hurting our marketing, and it isn't true to what we offer."*

Them: *"That label has been around for years. You marketing types always want to change the label."*

Me: *"I don't think we should change it just for the sake of change. But take a close look. We want to show how our water comes from a single, protected spring in Arkansas, right?"*

Them: *"Of course."*

Me: *"Can anyone tell me where the snow-capped mountains are here in Arkansas?"*

Them: (silence)

Me: "And by the way, our water doesn't come from a river. Rivers are filled with stuff that comes out of fish . . . not exactly the message of purity."

Them: "When can you come up with a new design?"

We will never know whether that specific logo image had actually hurt business. But we do see plenty of examples where even small slices of inauthenticity cause big problems. Domino's Pizza Inc. designed a smartphone app to show its customers, in real time, a to-the-minute description of their pizza's production. This description includes the name of each Domino's employee handling and delivering the order. That feature proved popular with customers such as 24-year-old Brent Gardiner, who at times used the feedback feature to send his personal encouragement. Things changed when a man he happened to know showed up to deliver his pizza—after the app specified that someone named "Melinda" would be doing the honors. That tiny lie—or at least the perception of a lie—had an, ahem, domino effect on the company's credibility. As Mr. Gardiner was quoted in *The Wall Street Journal,* "Ever since then, I knew everything they said, I felt, was made up."

While the absence of authenticity can damage customer relationships, the presence of it can boost growth. A research team of professors from Yale, Stanford, and Columbia studied restaurants and determined the connections between customers' perceptions of authenticity and how many stars they offered in reviews. They controlled for other factors (such as ratings of food quality). The restaurants with high authenticity ratings earned high overall ratings, often by a half star or more. That tends to translate into 3 to 6 percent higher revenues.

But for the all-time record-setting example of using raw authenticity to sell a lot more prepared foods, look no farther than Charlotte McCourt. The eleven-year-old Miss McCourt had begun her annual campaign to sell the most Girl Scout Cookies in her small troop; she hoped to match the 300 boxes of cookies she had sold the previous year. She heard her father Sean mention that a longtime friend of his was pretty wealthy. Less than an hour later, Sean noticed in his Sent folder that his daughter had emailed the rich friend.

In my neighborhood, the Girl Scouts typically use a cute sales message along the lines of, "You know my parents, and it's cookie time, so please buy your cookies from me." Charlotte did something very different; she offered her personal rating, on a 1 to 10 scale, of each Girl Scout cookie variety. Her honesty was refreshing and hilarious. Some of the cookies received personal ratings of "9" on the 1–10 scale with descriptions like *inspired.* Others were subject to brutal honesty. Charlotte used words and phrases such as *unoriginality, blandness,* and *bleak, flavorless, gluten-free wasteland.* Through her remarkable message, this young girl instinctively built trust by showing she was willing to lose all or part of a sale.

How, you might ask, did we learn about an email from an eleven-year-old Girl Scout? As it turns out, Sean the dad works with the popular TV host and producer Mike Rowe on Rowe's podcast "The Way I Heard It." Sean showed the email to Rowe—who liked it so much that he read it on his Facebook page. Charlotte shut down her website after selling 26,086 boxes of cookies and donating 12,430 of them— what the Girl Scouts affirmed as an all-time record. In his video, between belly laughs, Rowe said, "A basic tenet of sales is that you can't sell a product unless people first trust you. The best way to get them to trust you is to tell the truth."

TAKE A MANAGER MOMENT . . .

- Examine your website, videos, and any other messages that are going out to the marketplace. Which words and phrases are most common? (Can you make a Top Ten list?)

- Compare the words and phrases you are using right now to those your top two or three competitors are using. Do you sound like them, or are you different?

- Now compare the words and phrases you are using right now to the list of words that generally get the most traction. Are there specific words that might need changing?

3

GETTING RELEVANT:
What Customers and Prospects Actually Want (and Need) to Hear

THE GREAT FOOTBALL COACH Lou Holtz once said, "Never tell your problems to anyone. Twenty percent don't care and the other 80 percent are glad you have them."

That's funny yet also uncomfortably true, at least in our everyday lives. But when it comes to business messaging, things are a bit different. It is more likely that 80 percent (or more) of consumers don't care about your challenges. That has little to do with you—and a lot to do with consumers' general mindset.

Approximately half of Americans say they don't have enough time to do the things they want. According to Frank Newport, editor-in-chief of the Gallup Poll, there isn't much new here; that proportion has held pretty steady—within a few percentage points either way—for several decades. That means half of the marketplace is feeling a regular sense of scarcity. When people feel that their time is scarce, they tend to lose patience and turn inward even more than usual.

We have technology to potentially alleviate the time pressure, yet that same technology can also be part of the problem. Many of us are drowning in inputs and information but are still thirsty for a sense of direction. We are stuck in a pattern of always-on, anytime and anywhere. It is a phenomenon that the consultant, author, and former high-tech executive Linda Stone terms "continuous partial attention." Motivated by a fear of missing something, millions of people are hooked on the brain buzz that comes from feeling connected. Unfortunately, that hook also keeps those people in a relatively constant stressed-out state.

As Ms. Stone puts it on her website, "We are so accessible, we're inaccessible. The latest, greatest powerful technologies have contributed to our feeling increasingly powerless."

You and I cannot fix that. Nor should we try to "fix" anyone. But we do need to fully appreciate how and why so many of the people in our audience lack the proclivity to connect. It is on us to find the right approach.

THE PAINFUL TRUTH: MOST PEOPLE DON'T WANT TO HEAR ABOUT YOU

Think back to the last time you attended a crowded party or big event. Was there a time when you were chatting with someone else and felt like that person was losing interest and looking for the next person (or drink) with which to engage? You likely weren't the issue. Nevertheless, it is a frustrating feeling.

Politicians are known as the poster children for this type of behavior. At rallies, fundraisers, or meetings they might appear to have the attention span of a ferret—always looking for the next hand to shake. The notable exceptions have used the power of personal attention and have been very successful.

I have lived in Arkansas for nearly two decades. It's a state whose population is less than that of Los Angeles—so it is common here to run into political and business leaders, and often to know them on a first-name basis. Along the way I have had the opportunity to spend a bit of time with both Bill Clinton and Mike Huckabee. If you pay any attention to politics, then you know these two individuals are very accomplished but with very different political views; Mr. Clinton, a Democrat, was the 42nd President of the United States and Mr. Huckabee, a Republican, was a presidential candidate, TV host, and best-selling author. Both served as governor of Arkansas.

What these men share are a couple of qualities that set them apart from nearly every other political leader that I have come across. During face-to-face conversation—which is typically in a group setting or at an event—both can muster an intense focus on the other person and make that person feel, in the moment, that he or she is the most interesting and important person on the planet. Both men have, if not literally "photographic" memories, something pretty close. (One of Governor Huckabee's staff members told me, "He can get interrupted by someone he hasn't seen in months or years, and remember the name of their hunting dog.")

Remarkable, right? I strongly suspect this capacity for connection is a key reason why two very different men, both born in the tiny hamlet of Hope, Arkansas (population of maybe 10,000), went on to national fame and great political success.

Most of us—myself included—don't have such conversational focus (and aren't running for anything). It's often the case that we are on the other side of the equation. Perhaps it's at an event, or in a meeting, or on a phone call.

Someone else is speaking, and . . . our attention wanders. The conversation doesn't feel immediately relevant, and your mind jumps to something or someone else. It's a natural response, given the number of competing inputs and priorities. Our default focus is typically on ourselves. This natural tendency makes it difficult for your business message—no matter how important and valuable it may be—to break through.

Consumers have the upper hand—and they know it. We see evidence of their empowerment across settings and industries. Friends who are interior designers, architects, and builders tell me that many customers get immersed in Houzz, Pinterest, HGTV, and many magazines and home fashion catalogs. The implication is that homeowners are less dependent on their designers for ideas. They get the ideas on their own, then compare potential designers—if they decide they even need one—on price and terms. That means a creative business is being dragged into commoditization, with the result of lower success rates in selling design services and downward pressure on fees.

When your consumer audience feels more powerful, their focus turns even more inward. An interesting experiment illustrates the point. Imagine you were given a marker and asked to draw an uppercase "E" on your own forehead. (No, it isn't a Sharpie or any sort of permanent marker.) Basically, there are two ways to do so. The first would be to draw the E as if you were looking at what you draw, in which case the E would appear to face backward for anyone looking at you. The other way would be to draw the E in the direction that others could read it. I suppose this is a bit like the sports fans who paint their faces, arms, or chests for the big game!

A research team led by Adam Galinsky used this simple exercise to test whether feeling powerful in the moment affects our perspective. The team gathered a group of participants and first asked everyone to write a short essay; half of them wrote about a high-power experience while the others wrote about a low-power experience. Next they were asked to "as quickly as you can, draw a capital E on your forehead." Those who were randomly assigned to the high-power condition were nearly three times more likely to draw the E in the self-oriented direction.

As consumers feel more and more power, their natural self-focus will only grow. Of course, the desire to talk about ourselves is no modern phenomenon. It turns out to be a brain thing.

THERE'S CHEMISTRY: WHY IT FEELS SO GOOD TO TALK ABOUT OURSELVES

For most people, their own ideas and stories dominate the conversation. On average, people spend about 60 percent of their conversations talking about themselves. The tendency is even more pronounced—about 80 percent—in social media communications. Presumably, the difference on Twitter or Facebook is that we can't notice other people losing interest.

Are we all a bunch of out-of-touch narcissists? The answer is simple and, thankfully, forgiving. Research tells us that we talk about ourselves because our brains make it feel good.

Princeton University psychologist Diana Tamir led a research study to uncover some causes. The team found that, when research participants were prompted to talk about themselves, several areas of their brains became more activated. Among them were two brain regions in the mesolimbic dopamine system that have been linked to the feelings of pleasure also associated with good food and even sex. We are almost inexorably drawn to the habit of talking about ourselves because it feels so good.

Building the discipline to talk about others as much as ourselves is, for many of us, akin to eating more broccoli and less cake. (You can make your own comparison when it comes to sex.)

If it's only natural for the "I"s to have it in most conversations, how can we still excel in getting other people interested? There can be times when a professional can lead with "I" and do so very effectively, such as:

- "I know." Sometimes you can (and should) assert a fact or concept. Try saying "I know" rather than the slightly weaker "I believe" or "I think"; you will project more confidence. This doesn't make you a know-it-all but instead underscores your specific expertise. Just make sure you are indeed correct, because these days anyone can fact-check you in seconds with the swipe of a finger.

- "I feel." This one can certainly be overdone; some people focus on their feelings to a degree that chases others away from the conversation! But an appropriate discussion of what you are sensing (e.g., "I'm feeling more optimistic about this deadline," or "I sense some extra frustration out of the Western region team") can help you test assumptions and perhaps learn something new. It can also help you to be better understood. Others might argue your facts or conclusions, but no one can argue your feelings.

- "I recommend." You saw this one in the previous chapter. A recommendation—based on your experience as well as your understanding of someone else's situation—is stronger than a "suggestion" and far better than tossing out some options without any guidance. As a buyer, I pay attention to recommendations from people who know their stuff and also understand the specifics of my situation.

If you are at least aware of the whole mesolimbic dopamine system thing, then you and your team can harness it appropriately—having your conversational cake and eating it too.

SO LET'S GET ENGAGED (WITH OUR AUDIENCES, THAT IS)

For business and marketing leaders, customer "engagement" is a common mantra. As mantras go, it's a laudable one. Engagement means there is interest from customers or prospects to hear more and then begin some sort of dialogue. In the nonbusiness, matrimonial use of "engagement," conversations lead to mutual lifetime commitment.

Building engagement—even the less profound, more professional variety—might require a shift in your messaging strategy in at least a couple of ways. First, you and your team will need to be consistently vigilant to keep your focus on the outside. It is all too easy to talk about ourselves. Those brain chemicals in our customers' heads (as well as our own) can collectively act as a sort of rip current, pulling us away from each other. But even when our language is appropriate and interesting to customers, we might need to adjust a second component: timing. Simply put, *when* is it best to try to engage potential customers (or clients, or members, or donors, or whomever might be willing to fork over some of their money)?

There is plenty of research confirming that buyers today engage sellers later (if at all) in their decision-making processes. Buyers are doing their own research, reading reviews, and basically taking control of the conversation away from the seller. As you will see in Chapter 5, in many cases consumers seem to prefer the self-service route and do everything on their own. Not only does that frustrate us sellers, but often it doesn't work out well for the buyer either.

We can still manage to be engaging, and thus more influential, earlier in customers' decision-making cycles, but it takes some conversational work. The key is to offer our unique expertise or shed light on how relevant peers are approaching this type of decision, or otherwise guide customers to hold their horses long enough to see their decision in some new way.

How might you and your team build a more engaging set of conversations? Here are three lessons I've learned from my work with field sales, service, and business development teams:

- **Information is not the same as insight.** Some professionals assume they need to "educate" the buyer, then go too far by tossing around a bunch of disparate facts and figures. That does not serve the buyer's interests. We can all get overwhelmed with information. Engagement will both simplify data and make clear the implication of that data for the buyer.

- **Engagement includes emotion.** Being insightful is different than asking for pain points, then offering to ride to the rescue with your product. Instead, it means knowing enough about prospects to recognize their challenges and opportunities. That approach shows you are interested in the world of the buyer and willing to collaborate in solving problems.

- **You can provoke without being presumptuous.** Some sellers unfortunately try to demonstrate that they know more than the buyer does. During a recent engagement, a salesperson was demonstrating his approach during a role play. He kept saying things like "I know what you're thinking" and "We know exactly what you're considering." My guidance was that, even if those assertions happened to be true, the approach itself would likely turn off the prospect. Who wants to be told that they're just like everyone else? It's far better to say something on the order of "A pattern I've seen is . . . " or "Many of your peers say things to me like . . . "—which shows your smarts while still giving prospects enough oxygen to assert their individuality.

WHAT IS IT LIKE TO BE ENGAGED WITH YOU?

That feels like a simple question, doesn't it? Answering that simple question honestly might be more difficult than you think. It has been for me. Yet if we want to be engaging with customers, then don't we also owe it to them to understand what we are getting them into?

This is not a burning issue if your organization has a low-risk, low-price, and low-touch offering; customers aren't engaged in conversation with their favorite brand of dental floss. But if you're offering something that is personally meaningful, of higher value, and/or potentially confusing (meaning that there is actual evaluation and decision making involved), then these are important considerations.

I see three major categories of results from those professionals and organizations who engage effectively:

- **Their customers feel smarter.** They report being more informed and having greater clarity for having engaged with those organizations. They received valuable insights and concepts that provided the right inputs for their decisions.

- **Their customers believe they were given sound advice.** Often the advice wasn't some dictate about what the result of their decision should be but instead guidelines on what a good decision-making process should look like for them.

- **Their customers feel valued.** They say the seller was approachable, responsive, and easy to buy from—in other words, a good egg.

Even if things seem to be going smoothly, it might be valuable to have an occasional checkup. I was speaking recently with my business adviser (yep, I have one myself) about some new service offerings. After he had examined my website and promotional plans, we had this conversation:

Adviser: Jim, you're making it difficult for prospects to decide to buy from you. It isn't clear enough how you can help them. They're having to do too much work.

Me: (uncomfortable silence)

Regardless of whether you have an adviser or a mentor, it also makes sense to have this conversation with existing customers or clients. Ask them questions that are easy to interpret and answer in their own words (not a long survey or checklist). Why do they like doing business with you? Are there any problems or opportunities in their business that you might be able to shed some light on? Then, just listen. Not only will you learn more about the language of your best customers, you will also show them how much you value the relationship.

DON'T WE ALL NEED SOMEBODY TO . . . TRUST?

Our audiences want to be offered relevant information, guidance, and encouragement. Yet even that list is a bit incomplete. If we're considering what they both want *and* need from us, then we must include a bit of the dark side. Everyone is carrying baggage stuffed with their versions of fears, anxieties, and anticipated disappointment. As a business owner and therapist friend of mine once told me, "There is only one fear: the fear that you will hurt me." Where can consumers find comfort that they won't get hurt?

Edelman, the global public relations and communication agency, prepares its annual Edelman Trust Barometer in order to gauge trust in government, the media, and other institutions. Suffice to say that trust has taken a beating in recent years. Businesses across much of the globe have to operate in an environment of increasing skepticism and disconnection.

There are nuggets of good news. Business in general rates higher than do most other sectors. In the 2018 survey, slightly more than half (52 percent) of the general population, and 64 percent of those Edelman calls the "informed public," place some degree of trust in business. And if it's *your* business, then things are even a bit better. Worldwide, 72 percent of employees tend to trust their employer. As a business professional, you have the opportunity to establish trust in your communities and especially within your organization, but you cannot rely on some broad high tide of public sentiment to lift you. It will take some work. The buying decisions that seem like easy slam dunks to you might risk opening a bag of anxieties for the human being doing the buying.

For decades, economists assumed that people acted as "rational agents" when making decisions, with a sober evaluation of potential wins and losses. Over time, we have come to understand the ways that real people making real decisions depart from that assumption. We are not objective, dispassionate decision makers—whether for ourselves or our businesses. That doesn't mean we are wrong, but only human.

Recently, a client began moving to a different business model. Because of this initiative, their customers will eventually have to buy their services in a different way. The services are popular and customers have been loyal; repurchase and renewal rates have historically been higher than 90 percent.

The company's leaders believe strongly that their new model is best for everyone. They defined the value proposition, made an aggressive discount offer to early adopters, and proactively called on their customer base. To their surprise and dismay, a sizable proportion of customers had either declined the offer to switch altogether or delayed a decision.

Why would otherwise satisfied customers, who are already in the habit of re-upping, now be deciding not to decide? The answer is in a powerful psychological force called "loss aversion."

Loss aversion was first unearthed by Daniel Kahneman (with his research cohort, the late Amos Tversky) beginning in the late 1970s. The only psychologist to win a Nobel Prize in economic science, Dr. Kahneman showed in his book *Thinking, Fast and Slow* that two systems are involved in the way we think. System 1 is fast, emotional, and intuitive; System 2 is slower and more logical. The eye-opener was how influential System 1 thinking is in many decisions. One major pattern is that losses affect us more than do gains (about twice as much).

Back to the company with the new business model. What was going on? Well, as much as people talk about the need for change in the abstract, they generally don't like making changes themselves—especially if it feels like the change is being forced on them. In this case, the change customers were presented with meant a departure from their habits (which were working just fine, judging from the high renewal and repurchase rates). Customers were paying more attention to the downside, defaulting to indecision and unwilling to pull the trigger.

A couple of years prior, the seller had set an internal goal to be seen by its customers as a "trusted adviser." This experience was a wake-up call for them. They decided to slow down and change their customer conversations. They are offering more time for customers to consider the best path. Rather than lead with an assumed value proposition and pushing for a decision, they create an environment with the potential to uncover assumptions, objections, and anxieties.

THE THREE STEPS TO BEING A TRUSTED PROFESSIONAL

My wife and I have three sons, so it's a treat when we get to have a date night. On those occasions when we go out to dinner, I have noticed two different patterns in how my wife typically speaks with our server compared to the way I generally do. For my part, I tend to gloss over the specials but might ask what is popular (which reveals my own leaning toward social proof), or how a certain dish is prepared (as if I would really know the difference). My wife, on the other hand, will often ask our server (whom we will likely have known for mere seconds), "What do you like?"

At first, my wife's approach made little sense. Everyone has different tastes, leanings, and sensitivities when it comes to food—so how would the favorites of a stranger be useful to making one's own choices? Because Alison is an unusually kind and warm person, I figured her questions were a way to be social rather than a diagnostic device to make a better choice of entrée.

But when I gave this more thought, I realized that her brief exchanges are rooted in some messaging truths. You might have already caught on to her use of the word *you*— perhaps the most powerful word in persuasion, as we saw in Chapter 2. That puts the server in position of authority, yes, but it also makes the conversation more personal. The server wants to offer good advice that will reflect on him or her and surely doesn't want to deal with a guest who followed a recommendation and then wasn't happy.

Here's the way a recent exchange went:

Wonderful Wife: "What do you like?"

New Friend Server: "I like most everything on the menu, but I probably get the shrimp pasta most often for myself. Now, it's a little spicy but I like spicy food."

Wonderful Wife: "I'm not into spicy food as much. Could I get it less spicy?"

New Friend Server: "I'm sure we could, but I'll check with the chef."

The server answered the question but also—to hedge her bet—added that she has a preference for spicy foods that others might not share. Then she became the means for Alison getting something she would enjoy but that is a little different than the standard preparation. Everybody wins.

Millions of business professionals have a consultative element in what they offer. Consultants and coaches certainly do, but investment advisers, attorneys, designers, architects, stylists, clothiers, restaurateurs, and many, many others do as well. Their expertise and guidance are an important—perhaps the most important—component of their offerings. If that describes your work, even in part, then how can you build trustworthiness?

Based on my experience plus some great research into consumer psychology, I find that prospective clients have to answer two questions for themselves before granting you their trust: "Do you know what you're doing?" and "Will you work in my best interest?" The first question is about your expertise, whereas the second gets to the fuzzier issue of empathy.

When confident the answers are yes, those prospective clients' belief system elevates to something like "They are experts, and good people. I believe that they will carefully consider my needs and keep up with needs as they change. They won't treat me like part of a herd and won't give me the same advice they'd give anybody else. They are not going to pass my work off to a junior person or outsource it to someone who doesn't understand what I need. They wouldn't sell me a product that wasn't appropriate for me, just because it's profitable for them." That is certainly what we want clients and prospects to believe. To get there, professional service providers must work in sequence through three levels of competency—and avoid two traps in the sequence.

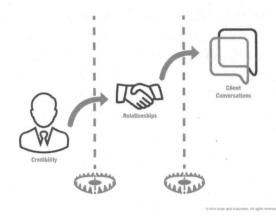

The first and most basic level involves *building credibility*. This is the realm of credentials, certification, and experience— attributes that show up on résumés and are searchable online when potential clients do their homework on you. Credentials are a relatively easy thing to communicate through marketing. Yet these days your credentials are considered "table stakes," or minimum requirements, by many prospects. The first Trustworthiness Trap I have seen is the belief that credibility alone is enough to earn trust and grow the business.

The second level involves *developing relationships*. Many professionals say theirs is a "relationship business," and they aren't necessarily wrong. On the other hand, I also hear from professionals who are frustrated with their prospect lists. One recently said about a longtime friend who pledged her business to a competing firm, "She likes us but is not going to invest with us." You can have healthy personal rela- tionships that never develop into business or referrals. The second Trustworthiness Trap is the belief that having rela- tionships, even seemingly strong ones, will necessarily drive growth. In order to leap over that trap, you need to activate those relationships—for yourself and across the business.

The third and highest level involves *mastery of conversations*. At this level, everyone close to your business (e.g., employees, current clients, those who can provide referrals) knows how to talk about the business. Everyone is equipped with brief, conversational language and stories to share, whether the opportunity is at a business conference, networking event, regular client meeting, or a social conversation in the stands at a game. It is only through conversations that you can demonstrate that necessary quality of empathy, thus activating your relationships and putting your expertise to its best use. This highest level is the space where you can ease customers' anxieties and demonstrate that you will be working in their best interests.

These three levels represent a progression for business growth, with each new level building on the previous one. Ultimately you and your colleagues can become credible, competent experts plus relationship builders plus skilled leaders of the client conversation.

YOUR MESSAGE HELPS THE PROCESS

A true message manager does not simply don the clothing of false empathy in order to get customers to like us. Rather, we understand the reality that our customers (and future ones) are getting trampled by information and could use our help. Despite—or possibly because of—modern technology, decisions are taking longer, involving more people, and are less satisfying. That problem isn't going away.

Research into B2B (business-to-business) buyers is finding, for example, that at the same time the process of researching and buying complex solutions has never been easier, the people doing the buying are feeling overwhelmed and stressed. They also second-guess themselves a lot after the purchase. A research team led by Nicolas Toman of the Corporate Executive Board studied more than 600 such buyers; they found that buyers are asking themselves, "Would another choice have been better?" more than 40 percent of the time. It's tough to go through one's professional life carrying a bunch of regret baggage.

You can help. First, you need to get your message (signal) above the noise. But even more profoundly, there is power in your message to lower others' anxiety, help them decide how to decide, and offer them a trustworthy source in a world where such sources feel increasingly rare. That can only come through a conversation that works for both sides.

The next chapter is about the best conversational strategies and tactics for different situations, including stories, pictures, questions, and even numbers. But no multiplication tables.

TAKE A MANAGER MOMENT . . .

- Who is an ideal customer or client for your organization? Think in terms of the things they are doing today, what they want, and what they need.

- Write it down for yourself, and also ask some of your colleagues. Do your assumptions match?

- Once your team has reached some consensus on your ideal customers, write down the most important pressures those future customers are likely feeling when it comes to your type of offering (e.g., not enough time to think about it, financial stress, too many options to consider, have to get agreement from others). Now come up with some questions and insights that would help create the right conversational environment.

4

CRAFTING YOUR CONVERSATIONS:
What Needs to Be Said . . . and How!

"I HAVE BEEN WORKING on this thing so long that now I'm lost."

Scott, a regional sales manager for a manufacturer, was an up-and-comer. He had earned a reputation not only for hitting his sales numbers but also for his innate messaging skills. Scott had a knack for asking good questions and simplifying complex technical details. Recently elevated to a manager role, he was showing promise in the way he worked with reps to help them do the same.

Because of his rising reputation, he had been asked to create two very different types of messages. The first was a capabilities presentation, one that eventually salespeople across the company could use in meetings with prospects' finance leaders. The second was a set of talking points for everyone to reference at a big trade show, one where the company would have a major (and expensive) presence on the show floor. Essentially, the company's leadership saw skills in Scott that they hoped to "clone" for dozens of reps and thousands of conversations. They asked me to check in with Scott. What I found was one frustrated manager.

He had run into a wall. The conversational skills that Scott had been using so well—and even coaching to others—were, for some reason, not kicking in. Scott had spent hours on the project but had little to show for it. He asked, "Am I overthinking this?"

This was a new type of challenge for Scott, one with a lot of opportunity for both him personally and the company as a whole. "I feel like I'm about to blow it," he said. "The leadership is counting on me, and all of a sudden I'm questioning the things that I thought I already knew how to do."

Scott had been approaching this project in what seemed a logical way. He would begin by drafting the capabilities presentation in Microsoft PowerPoint, then lift the strongest bullet points and proof statements as the talking points everyone could use at the big trade show. And therein was the source of Scott's frustration. He was thinking of the medium first, rather than envisioning great conversations and building back from there. It is a common, almost expected, approach. You can do better.

I used the phrase "and how!" in this chapter's title with two ideas in mind. First, people have for generations said "and how!" with enthusiasm to express their strong agreement. You have something to say that is worth agreement, right? Second, let's talk about "how" to get there—even in a marketplace full of noise and where most of your audience is predisposed to tune you out.

YOUR CONVERSATION IS NOT A PRESENTATION

Most businesses that I see—especially the larger ones—have The Deck. It is a stock presentation about the organization, carefully prepared and vetted, that everyone is supposed to use. New employees are subjected to this presentation during their onboarding. Sales and account representatives are to use it to educate current and prospective customers. The corporate communications or public relations teams might use it with the media as well as community organizations. It is meant to drive consistency and thus reinforce the corporate brand. It tells the world everything the company presumes the world needs to know.

Most versions of The Deck that I have seen look remarkably similar. The title slide shows a picture of headquarters, an urban skyline, or a stock photo of happy-looking employees. Next there is a vision or mission statement. Perhaps there is a timeline of the company's history. Then there is a description of the company's size, growth, locations, and product lines. Sound familiar?

The other thing that's remarkably similar about these presentations is the reaction to them. Almost no one likes them. The presenters generally like the professional look of The Deck but . . . well, they want to tailor it a bit for their own purposes. They take matters into their own keyboards by rearranging and modifying slides. After a while, there might be several versions of the supposedly unifying message throughout the organization. For their part, audiences know what to expect in these presentations; they tune out until they hear that wonderful line, ". . . and on my last slide."

If the prototypical PowerPoint presentation isn't meeting anyone's needs very well, then let's consider different ways of sharing your organizational story. How about we tell a story? You likely have plenty of raw material, readily available, to craft the type of story that is fun to tell, interesting to hear, and ultimately persuasive. You might just need to shake up the format.

Many companies rely on published case studies as a primary means to create and share stories. One client has nearly 500 case studies on its website, many of which run well over 2,000 words. That represents a lot of work from the marketing team and a treasure trove for anyone who talks with customers. The problem with those case studies, as is commonly the case, was that the sales teams weren't using them.

Case studies, when used as part of customer conversations, can help prospects understand the value of your offerings and lessen the perceived risk of buying your stuff. Most case studies I've seen are full of information, stay true to brand messaging guidelines, and are professionally produced (they look great!). The bad news is that case studies absorb resources, are typically committee creations, and can read with all the pizzazz of an unflavored rice cake. A more conversational version of that same story should have prospective buyers on the edge of their seats—bringing the audience into the emotions of the situation and leading them to root for the protagonist.

Here's an example. A company in the flash-storage business had developed a set of case studies that illustrated its advantage in speed. One story described a customer in rail-shipping logistics who needed faster batch-order processing in order to optimize shipments. After the customer bought the new solution and began using it, they did indeed process orders much faster. The case study described the what, why, and how of that success with the equivalent of, "We installed the Super Platinum Batchinator 3000X [I made that up] and processing time was decreased, saving money and improving customer service." Nothing wrong there, except that the story was not translating to customer conversations.

I spoke with the person who actually sold that deal. How did that customer come to believe his problem was lack of speed? In quite vivid language he described the general manager's frustration. "He would arrive at the office early, and then his people would come in but they wouldn't start doing anything. They would be at the coffeemaker or the watercooler." The datacenter responsible for overnight processing of the previous day's data was often overwhelmed. Until the system could catch up and produce schedules, no one could begin their day's work. "The GM was thinking his people were lazy or distracted. 'They're not showing up ready to work!' he would say, and then stomp around the office." I could visualize that manager looking around and seeing 100 people wasting time every morning. We can almost feel the churn in his stomach. It probably wasn't much fun for those 100 employees, either.

Now it became much easier to share the underlying emotion in this story. The sales team learned to talk about the true story of a manager starting most workdays with stress and frustration. Then they could show how the problem wasn't the people; the problem was the system. The prospective customers (managers themselves) could easily relate.

To find the conversation starters in your case studies, look for the pulse. Someone is trying to get somewhere, to achieve a goal, in the face of difficult obstacles. What's the gap between the starting point and the landing point? Which emotions (both positive and negative) are involved? What were the surprises along the path?

It is definitely worthwhile to find and hone customer stories this way if you want to differentiate yourself. According to a Forrester survey, only 21 percent of executive-level buyers said that vendor salespeople "have relevant examples or case studies to share with me." That means about four-fifths of salespeople . . . got nothin'.

The published versions of case studies are still valuable. In my experience, they are best used as preparation for a conversation or as a follow-up (to provide detail) rather than as a substitute for the conversation. Your customer stories won't actually be shared around a campfire . . . but could they be?

YOUR CONVERSATION IS NOT AN INTERROGATION, EITHER

During my time as a corporate chief marketing officer, I had a budget for things such as advertising and public relations services, an annual distributors' conference, and packaging and label production. Potential vendors, sniffing for available budget dollars, would frequently call; they asked that I make time for a meeting to talk over our needs and their capabilities. I would generally try to make the time available. Good vendors are valuable, and you never know where the next useful idea could come from.

The reality was often disappointing. Either I would get talked to (with that company's version of The Deck) or, more commonly, I would be subjected to a barrage of questions. It often felt as though I was being deposed. To complete the picture, there was typically a junior associate present for the meeting—dutifully taking notes as if he or she were the court stenographer.

To a degree I was sympathetic. Ours was a mid-sized private company, so there was not as much information available to the outside world as would be the case for a large public company. Despite the information available on our website, or the content of press releases and interviews we had given about the business, it might be difficult to discern the details of our strategy.

Soon the time came to conduct a formal search process for an advertising agency. I tried to head off any confusion or wasted efforts by preparing a detailed description of our industry niche, business model, and growth strategies. During the search process, we allowed time for interested agencies to meet with our team in person for follow-up questions. Wouldn't you know it . . . several of the agencies that met with us asked questions that were already clearly covered in the description my team had spent hours preparing. And there was always a junior associate present taking more notes.

Today, there is even less excuse for subjecting customers to basic or needless questions. Anyone with a couple of hours and a web connection can do adequate homework on nearly any company or industry. Besides, most executives I know would rather hear your point of view than continue to repeat theirs.

In that same Forrester survey I mentioned earlier, executive-level buyers painted a harsh picture of the salespeople they deal with. They said 62 percent were knowledgeable about the products and services they sell—but 42 percent were knowledgeable about the buyer's industry and only 24 percent knew much about the buyer's specific business. And when the tables get turned during a sales conversation, just 30 percent of buyers said salespeople were "prepared for the questions that I ask."

You can be the refreshing exception. By recognizing the fundamental tensions and contradictions that your customers must deal with, you can create an environment for working together.

A LITTLE TENSION CAN BE OKAY

There is a lot of talk these days about storytelling. You might legitimately ask whether this is simply the latest business fad (such things do happen) or if something more fundamental is going on. Why not just educate buyers about what is possible if they do business with us? The answer is that recent research shows—at the neurochemical level—how stories affect activity in our brains.

Paul Zak has spent years studying brain activity, marketing, and management. He found, for example, that a neurochemical called oxytocin provides a signal in the brain that means "it's safe to cooperate with others." Stories can prompt the brain to release oxytocin, which in turn affects the degree to which people will help others or donate money to a charity tied to the narrative.

In his research, Zak proves that stories must develop tension in order to gain attention from the audience and ultimately affect behavior. Attention, he notes, is a scarce resource in our brains. But if a story can create tension, viewers and listeners actually begin to share the emotions of the characters and often mimick those feelings after the show is over.

Marketing might not be brain surgery, but with well-crafted stories it can be mind-altering.

THE BACKSTORY ABOUT STORIES

As long as we have brains on the brain, let's talk about how one of the oldest parts of our brains might play a key role in your messaging success.

The amygdala are a pair of almond-sized lumps near the brain stem that formed much of our earliest thinking as humans. By comparison, our "gray matter" (the cerebral cortex) is much newer.

Seth Godin, the entrepreneur and author, refers to the amygdala as our Lizard Brains. Godin says the functioning of our Lizard Brains is the underlying reason we often manage to sabotage our own progress (especially as we come closer to the end of a project or product launch).

The Lizard Brain is about fear, hunger, anger, desire, and emotional consolidation. Because of it we shy away from the unknown, the threatening, those things that might put us in a compromising position. We learn which people and circumstances put us at risk, then subconsciously steer clear of them in the future. We try too hard to fit in.

If your cerebral cortex—the New Brain—is built for higher-level analysis, verbal fluency, and innovation, then the Lizard Brain is all about avoiding uncomfortable stuff.

Remember this: the Lizard Brain is not equipped to process language. Words and text are only appropriate for the newer parts of our brains. That's why the simple and ancient act of drawing pictures is receiving new attention in our digital age. We are finding that the mere acts of writing things out, and drawing pictures of information you need to remember, will improve your memory. That should help you be more persuasive and effective.

One research group led by Jeffrey Wammes carried out a simple yet illustrative test to determine how people might best learn and recall lists of words. Participants received a list of words that could be drawn easily (such as *apple*), were told to either draw the word or write it out repeatedly, and were later asked to recall as many words from the list as possible in just one minute.

How did it go? The people who drew pictures typically recalled more than twice as many as those people who wrote words out over and over. In subsequent tests, the team confirmed that drawing a picture to represent a word was more effective than writing the word repeatedly, creating a mental image of the word, or viewing pictures of the object depicted by the word. Don't consider yourself an artist? The quality of the drawings did not matter.

I find that the act of drawing simple pictures is transformative for helping clients remember important facts or concepts. For example, our DSG Consulting clients for messaging projects get a customized whiteboard conversation tool. (I've seen salespeople draw their visuals in settings well beyond whiteboards—including on cocktail napkins, scorecards, and even an airsickness bag.) A client's CEO told me recently, "Even when I don't actually draw out our story on a whiteboard, I have that picture in my mind—and it keeps me on track within that conversation."

Here is another practical way that writing things out could be valuable to you or someone you know. If your child, grandchild, or friend is heading off to college, then you can help them dramatically improve their note-taking habits. Research by Pam Mueller and Daniel Oppenheimer found that writing—yes, writing—their notes longhand is more effective than tapping out notes into a computer.

In a series of three studies, the researchers found that students who took notes on laptops did worse on conceptual questions than did those who took notes longhand. Sure, the students who tapped out their notes could go faster and record more raw material for the tests, but they often were just transcribing the professor's words verbatim rather than processing the ideas. The students who wrote longhand tended to listen, digest, and summarize. That gave them an advantage in understanding and recall.

For you and your team, it makes sense to prepare (and actually write out) conversation plans in advance of customer meetings. That will help everyone to be more effective in the moment than if they had just read over product information or the PowerPoint deck. Keep some pens and paper around.

WAIT . . . THERE'S MATH? HOW TO USE NUMBERS AND STATISTICS

Which numbers do you believe these days? Are your customers and prospects of a similar mindset?

Marketers, pollsters, meteorologists, economic forecasters, and many other professionals face a rising tide of skepticism when they try to inform and persuade via statistics. Some of the damage has been self-inflicted when people who are in the description business have ventured into the prediction business. That is foolish.

Still, skepticism about statistics and claims has been growing for some time—across industries and national borders. As just one example, a Nielsen Global Survey found that people around the world are skeptical about the health claims found on food packaging (e.g., "low fat" or "all natural"). More than two-thirds of respondents believed nutritional claims are either never trustworthy or only sometimes trustworthy.

Businesspeople need to understand data and use it to communicate effectively with consumers, regulators, and the media. How can you make your case, clearly and honestly, in such a skeptical age? Here are three important considerations when using statistics to educate and persuade:

- **Use the right communication tools.** Mathematical literacy and attention are typically in short supply, so keep it brief. I have seen people stuff ten statistics into a single PowerPoint slide or a few dozen into an article or whitepaper. The audience is quickly overwhelmed. It's a better idea to focus on one or two statistics at a time.

Some ideas are easier to convey through statistics than are others. In that Nielsen survey, the most trusted health claims on food packaging were calorie counts, vitamin content, and fat content—things that appear to consumers as scientific, objective, and easily measured. On the other hand, consumers generally don't believe more ambiguous claims such as "freshness" and "heart-healthy" (only 15 percent of respondents thought those types of claims are always accurate).

Graphs, bar charts, and infographics convey authority and credibility. Consider using them, especially if you have a more complex, ambiguous idea to support.

• **Match your data to common understanding and personal experiences.** Many organizations try to use statistics to educate some segment of the public. But what if the public doesn't understand? The Nielsen survey found that only 41 percent of consumers around the world even "mostly understand" nutritional labels.

Part of the solution is to take data from a rather dry context (product labels) and connect it to more everyday experiences. For example, health experts typically recommend that adults drink 64 ounces of water per day. On its own, that number is difficult to remember and apply. But when you instead recommend eight 8-ounce glasses or four half-liter bottles of water per day, the guidelines are easier to visualize.

Mona Chalabi, a data journalist, gave a TED Talk on statistics that included a great example. She demonstrated the average distribution of flu season by month through a hand-drawn chart. Rather than lines or bars, her chart featured six noses representing the months of October–March. The length of, um, stuff coming out of each nose represented the number of times that month was the peak of flu season in each year since 1982. The visual might be a bit cringe-inducing for some, but it is easily relatable for everyone.

- **Be clear about sources and limitations.** Many uncertainties are associated with polls and how to interpret them—including sampling (who was selected), response rates (how many participated), and the order and wording of questions. Each can introduce errors and biases. If you are transparent with the audience about the source of your statistics, then that act alone will blunt some skepticism.

HOW ABOUT THAT ELEVATOR PITCH?

I will freely state my bias: I don't like the term *elevator pitch.* That isn't necessarily because I floundered in an elevator-pitch competition.

The event was titled "Gone in 60 Seconds," a nice opportunity for entrepreneurs, investors, and otherwise interested parties to gather and network. It was held in an upscale bar; you can imagine that a lot of craft beers were consumed. Toward the end of the evening, a dozen or so startup businesses would give their elevator pitches, to be exactly one minute in length. (Snorkelers and swimmers would appear to have an advantage because they don't need to breathe as often as do the rest of us.) I was an investor in a startup business, and my colleagues thought I should be our representative for the pitch. How hard could this be?

My turn came toward the end of the schedule, as the bar was starting to run short of craft beers. The emcee handed me a microphone, showed me where the timer was located, and then pointed to me to begin. I started speaking. Five seconds later, my microphone began to work. A few people in the crowd (the ones paying attention and not gathered in the back of the room with their craft beers) shouted for me to start over. I did, but the timer did not. Despite my best effort to talkrealfastlikethis, I was Gone in About 46 Seconds.

These types of events have become popular, fueled in part by TV shows such as *Shark Tank* and the growth of speed-networking events. I appreciate the emphasis this trend puts on businesspeople knowing their value proposition and expressing it succinctly. But I have a caution, one that goes deeper than my own less-than-stellar performance one particular night. This same trend is debasing the more common, everyday, and valuable uses of your short story.

A one-way pitch is appropriate for pitch competitions or for an entrepreneur trying to find funding. But how often does that happen for you? For most professionals, it would be a waste of time to craft some seemingly great monologue that in reality isn't that interesting to others. On the other hand, it is quite valuable to have, at the ready, an interrelated set of short messages that naturally prompts interest and leads to a two-way conversation.

One of the very best at all this is Mark Levy. He helps clients of varying stripes—from executives and thought leaders to top entertainers—come up with positioning statements, stories, and pitches. I once heard Mark recommend a simple, fill-in-the-blank structure that might help you get started: "I help _____ to _____ which benefits them by _____."

Note how this structure almost forces someone to follow many of the proven guidelines for business messaging. It begins with "I" (it could be "we," of course) but then very quickly pivots to a focus on the type of customers you serve. There is little mention at the outset of specific products or services, but instead on what your business enables those customers to do and achieve. And, although you aren't going to sketch out a picture, the words you select can help people visualize for themselves what you do and whom you serve.

This structure is simple and valuable. However, it is neither automatic nor easy. As you have already seen, our brains will generally try to coerce our mouths to talk about ourselves. So, let's get a start on how you might fill in those blanks most effectively for your business.

The first blank gets to the specific marketplace need and type of customer you address. That could be defined by organization (such as mid-sized private firms, online retailers, or trade associations in the Midwest) and/or individual (professionals nearing retirement, first-time home buyers with a certain range of credit rating, or single African Americans). Use the "ideal customer" exercise at the end of the previous chapter. Make your description specific enough so that others can readily visualize that organization or individual for themselves.

The second blank addresses your "how." Do you provide a product that meets a need, offer a service that keeps your customers focused on what they do best, or train others to do something themselves? Is your help specific in time and to a project, or does it tend to be ongoing?

The third blank is about how your customers benefit. This is often stated as objective, prototypical results (e.g., the ROI you provide), the things your customers say, or the way you make your customers feel. If numbers are involved, limit yourself to one or two punchy ones.

A couple of examples I have heard are "Homeowners hire us so that they can have the best front yard in their neighborhood," and "I help mature companies stop being order takers, and start growing their revenue by 15 percent or more." You might not need to put all three components into one sentence. If you can state the ideal customer and their benefits in an interesting way, then the other person will very often ask you about the "how."

I recommend that you have an additional component ready, one that speaks to your customers' emotional benefits. It can help in a similar fashion as those customer stories. Be prepared to share what customers say—in their words. Do you have testimonials with great nuggets worth repeating? Your customers might have said that you "relieved stress" or "were super easy to work with." It isn't bragging if you say something on the order of "One client summed it up very well—he said we accomplished the things they knew they needed to do, and had even tried to start, but would never have finished on their own."

It can be difficult to find language that everyone can agree on (while keeping things brief). You will want help, both inside and outside of the organization. You will need to practice saying things out loud, because the interpretation of spoken words can be far different than if the same words were on a page or screen. It's very useful to set up buddy systems and have people role-play different conversational scenarios before they occur. But don't let any of this get you uptight. There is little if any downside. No one will be selling anything during an impromptu pitch or conversation—it's simply an added tool for building more growth opportunities.

That brings us back to Scott, the anxious sales manager who was in charge of putting together two important conversational tools. Scott ditched the PowerPoint for his capabilities presentation. Instead, we got a small team together to create a visual conversation that reps could learn. The audience of finance leaders has its own specific objectives, challenges, and hot buttons—so they would have little patience for waiting until slide 17 to talk about them.

For the trade-show talking points, it was a different matter. In that environment, there would be a much larger and more disparate group of people in attendance. Some might be potential buyers, whereas many others would just be kicking the tires. The corporate team would need something brief and easy to deliver, and that could progress in the moment into a dialogue for those who were interested. They decided on a form of that simple "pitch" structure, rather than the initial idea to copy talking points from a presentation. Both conversations proved very successful.

Now that you have begun to consider your message—including the words, stories, and formats that will work best—we should turn our attention next to your potential messengers. Who are they, where do they exist around your business, what do they need, and as a practical matter, what can we do for them?

TAKE A MANAGER MOMENT . . .

- With your ideal type of customer in mind, think of the most common and important major conversational scenarios (e.g., prospecting for a new customer, trying to gain additional business from an existing customer, or talking to a member about renewal). List three or four specific ones that would benefit from some written planning.

- Now for each think of (a) a customer story, (b) a simple picture, and (c) a statistic that would help your audience visualize the value of working with you. (You might not ultimately use all three, but the process will jump-start some brains!)

- Gather a group representing different parts of your organization. Put the phrase "I/We help _____ to _____ which benefits them by _____" on a whiteboard or flip chart. Ask everyone how they would fill in the blanks in a real conversation.

Part Two

A LOT MORE GREAT MESSENGERS

5

WE ARE ALL IN THIS:
Customer Conversations
Really Are for Everyone

SHARON INTRODUCED HERSELF TO ME as our team was setting up for a large training event. In her job, she supported the company's expansive sales and service teams; she had been doing this for nearly two years following her graduation from college. "There are several of us from the support team here. We don't actually talk to customers that much, but our boss thought it would be a good idea for us to hang out here and see what the sales teams are learning to say."

The training included small-group exercises and some role-play competitions. Over the course of the two days, a funny thing began to happen: the internal teams like Sharon's were adopting and presenting the new messages at least as well as were the sales teams. They got it! During a break on the second day, Sharon came up to me, smiled, and said softly, "I can do this as well as the sales guys!"

There are probably a lot of people around your organization who are like Sharon. They care about what the organization does and what others have to say about it. They might not know everything you do, or consider themselves to be great communicators, or be comfortable in knowing exactly what to say themselves. They might even need a nudge and some encouragement to join in to more customer conversations. But they probably have more inherent abilities than you—or they—realize.

Let's stipulate that company leaders—plus legions of gurus, writers, speakers, and other professional yappers— are prone to saying things like, "Everyone here is in customer service" or "We are all part of the sales team." Those statements are undoubtedly true, but they also run head-first into common assumptions and' practice. Typically, only a small percentage of people *behave* as if they are in sales or customer service regardless of where they reside on the organization chart. But there is lots of surprisingly good news, right in front of us, that can help move your teams much closer to that stated ideal. When that happens, growth follows.

EVERYONE IS A SALES REP

How much of your work time involves convincing or persuading people? Is it an hour in your typical workday? More? According to a study commissioned by Daniel Pink and reported in his book *To Sell Is Human: The Surprising Truth about Moving Others,* the average full-time American worker spends about 40 percent of his or her time in active persuasion mode. Pink calls this "non-sales selling." Furthermore, more Americans than you might think are involved in good old-fashioned "sales selling." Even during the rise of e-commerce since 2000—which has forced waves of disintermediation—the proportion of the U.S. workforce in sales (1 in 9) has stayed the same. A state comprised only of salespeople would be the fifth-most populous state in America!

Nevertheless, all of the platitudes in the world about "We're all selling something" will not sway everyone to embrace the idea. Many are downright uncomfortable with anything smacking of sales. Why? First, sales doesn't exactly have the best reputation as a profession. In national Gallup polling on the trustworthiness of various professions, "car salespeople" are always at or near the bottom (dwelling in the muck near "members of Congress" and "lobbyists"). During the past forty years, the combination of Americans who rate car salespeople "very high" or "high" in trustworthiness has never reached even 10 percent.

Another reason many pull back from the opportunities in non-sales selling is the belief that a distinct personality type (a type we don't think we have ourselves) is best suited for persuasion. Think backslapping, friendly, gregarious, hypersocial extraverts in sport coats. Depending on your age, the first image that comes to mind might resemble the Herb Tarlek character from the 1970s TV sitcom *WKRP in Cincinnati*, William H. Macy's Jerry Lundegaard car salesman character in the 1996 film *Fargo*, or the pushy young retail clerk who tried last month to sell you a service contract on a new gizmo. In any case, the image isn't flattering. Forty years after *WKRP* was airing on network TV—with an assist from syndication—Herb Tarlek remains an iconic symbol of the vacuous salesman in a bad polyester jacket.

Aside from the unprofessional look, the Tarlek-esque package contains a number of behaviors that make customers cringe. Salespeople are often accused of being overly concerned with their sales quota, not really listening to the customer, lacking social boundaries, and failing to ever take no for an answer.

I sometimes think of this prototypical blowhard to be like that person who pulls up next to you at a stoplight, singing loudly to a tune in their vehicle, seemingly oblivious to the world around them. It's amusing to see from afar, but I am also happy that I am not in that vehicle. That guy isn't going to let the environment stop him from enjoying the sound of his own voice.

The stereotype is not fair, of course. My work with dozens of organizations, including thousands of professional salespeople, has exposed me to the harsh reality of selling. It is tough and uncertain work, not for the faint of heart or thin of skin. When you're being told "no" on a regular basis, sent down organizational rat holes, lied to, and sometimes run through the procurement wringer just so that prospect can negotiate better terms from a competing vendor, you need a little bluster just to even things out. Many of us believe it's simply part of the mix when deploying the extraverts who are seemingly superior when it comes to selling. Perhaps the business world needs to change its collective thinking. Even if the entire business world doesn't, you certainly can.

I learned the hard way. While still in my twenties, I went into the small-market radio station business with an MBA classmate. Being inexperienced and naïve, I followed conventional wisdom. We would work the best advertiser accounts ourselves, then find some gregarious young people to work on commission and make a lot of calls to build additional business. After all, if sales success is a function of making more calls and pitching harder than the competition, then we could play that game as well as anyone.

The results were decidedly mixed. We grew the business but at a high cost of time, turnover, and frustration. When I investigated, I learned from our stations' customers (and the prospects we failed to land) that our gregarious young reps were often wearing out the market. They pitched, they pleaded, they persisted—but they didn't slow down long enough to listen. Over time we have learned how much more effective active listening is than incessant pitching. When businesspeople demonstrate active listening (through sensing, evaluating, and responding), they build trust and future business opportunities. My experience is that the business value of listening extends far beyond the sales team alone; it includes everyone with customer contact, including installation, service, delivery, and administrative teams. It also includes everyone else who knows about you and your business.

THIS IS FOR MORE THAN JUST A FEW EMPLOYEES . . . OR EVEN JUST EMPLOYEES

We hear a lot about the need for organizations to "join the social conversation." That advice is often directed to organizational leaders, pushing them to engage in the ever-growing list of social media channels (and often to hire expert help to avoid messing it up). Communication through social media is definitely important, and increasingly so. Unfortunately, however, in the rush to embrace social media and the online customer experience, some have lost sight of real-time customer interactions (or have put those concerns on the back burner). I find it is time for many to place more priority on the front lines of customer communication and even the so-called "back office" of the organization.

We know from experience—in business and as customers ourselves—what it's like when pitches, presentations, phone calls, retail shopping encounters, service calls, and the like go poorly. Good companies lose reputation, loyalty, and revenue. Because these frontline interactions are so numerous and common, it's also easy to take for granted how vital they are to business growth. As you saw in Chapter 1, some 93 percent of word of mouth happens offline—typically face to face. There's also mounting evidence that the skill with which your colleagues interact with customers during all of those encounters has substantial, measurable impact on the brand.

Think, for example, of the spectrum of encounters that customers have with frontline service employees—ranging from the more routine maintenance calls to bigger service problems. A research group led by Nancy Sirianni tested those scenarios to see what happens when customer conversations are (or are not) consistent with the company's overall brand personality. The research group created audio recordings, purportedly from a call center, involving both routine calls and problems; they manipulated whether the employees' words, tone, and direction were consistent with the companies' overall brand personality.

The results revealed that, when employees' customer interactions were consistent with company positioning, brand strength and consumers' willingness to pay more rose significantly. When the phone-center interactions were inconsistent, those same measures went south. The impact was even stronger for companies and brands that were not very well known. The researchers say the key factor for companies putting this to practical use is whether employees can "internalize elements of the brand positioning." In other words, do customer-facing employees believe in the company's value proposition, and are they equipped to convey it to customers?

That customer-facing team might not just be the sales team and the call center. One of my clients is an HVAC (heating, ventilation, and air conditioning) company, with multiple offices across a wide geographic area. They have two sales teams (one for commercial accounts, the other for residences), plus an in-house call center and dispatch team. This is a high-performing company, a leader in market share that generates consistently strong customer satisfaction scores. But they also want to grow faster, especially through new products and services beyond just the traditional air-conditioning units and furnaces.

As a starting point, we examined who was leading most of the customer interactions. We learned that more than 70 percent were from "techs," the service technicians who go to homes and offices to do the actual maintenance and troubleshooting work. These techs are dedicated, skilled problem solvers who have to deal with generally agitated customers in generally uncomfortable conditions (my "ride-along" experience with one tech included helping him deal with cluttered attic access, barking dogs, and a wasp nest on a 95-degree day). These workers carry the load when it comes to customer experience. They have the opportunity to also head off potential future problems (safety issues, equipment that is likely to fail) as well as to make the customer aware of other products and services. Yet typically these types of frontline employees get ignored internally; they aren't informed about the full range of products and services offered or what customers are buying these days.

Imagine the growth opportunities in a business like this one, if even 10 percent of a frontline employee's customer interactions led to an opportunity to sell other products or services (and my experience is that 10 percent is quite conservative). In this case, the 10 percent applied to 70 percent of all their customer conversations would produce 7 percent revenue growth—just by changing some elements of how techs talk with customers. Where would *you* get started?

Employees are typically at the core of your set of messengers, but they are far from the only group you can enlist to accelerate your business. My friends who manage nonprofits and professional associations tell me that much of their time and energy is dedicated to volunteers—finding, informing, and motivating them, plus coordinating their activities. These volunteers are often passionate yet distracted, balancing their day jobs and other commitments with the heartfelt desire to help out. Similarly, in the for-profit world companies can count retired employees (alumni), suppliers, distributors, and channel partners, plus other friends in the communities they serve, as potential messengers. People clearly like to talk. Their jobs and professional relationships consume a lot of their time, money, pride, reputation, anxiety, and planning. Why not allow your organization to be part of their natural conversations?

ALMOST EVERYONE HAS MESSENGER POTENTIAL

If some organizations limit the scope of potentially great customer conversations because they think according to narrow job descriptions like "sales," then others limit themselves with assumptions about the capacity and personality types of their potential messengers. The biggest limiting assumption is that the best potential messengers are necessarily the extroverts on your team.

If there is any long-held core belief system around selling, then it involves the advantages of extraversion; effective salespeople are assumed to be the ones comfortable with cold calls, networking, and basically any opportunity to pitch their wares. This belief has become the basis of a self-sustaining cycle. Extraverts are supposedly better at sales, so companies and managers screen applicants for sales jobs accordingly. Extraverts become the dominant proportion of the candidate pools, so they get hired for sales jobs at higher rates. Sales managers look for additional entry-level people who will fit into the existing culture, and so on.

Then again, if you ask people (in their role as consumers and buyers) about salespeople, you'll most often get that negative reaction reflected over time in those Gallup polls. Salespeople are viewed as arrogant, pushy, untrustworthy, poor listeners concerned only about the sale. That gap—separating business assumptions and consumers' experiences—is as wide as the Grand Canyon. Furthermore, a research team led by Murray R. Barrick did a combined analysis of 35 separate studies of actual salespeople; they found that the statistical relationship (correlation) between extraversion and sales performance was 0.07. That is, for all practical purposes, zero. The upshot is that managers could have been selecting salespeople on the basis of earlobe length rather than personality and done just as well. What gives?

Adam Grant of the Wharton School tested this relationship directly, with a group of actual salespeople. Professor Grant's team measured the personality traits of 340 reps in outbound-call centers, and then recorded their weekly revenue generation over a three-month period. The team also controlled for factors such as the number of hours worked and the number of months on the job. The extraverts did produce a slightly higher hourly revenue than did the introverts, but it wasn't a practical difference. This result alone is a splash of cold water on any Herb Tarlek–inspired assumptions about outgoing salespeople. But what was really interesting were the results from call center reps who were neither pure extraverts nor pure introverts.

As it turns out, the people who are best at sales and persuasion are neither extraverts nor introverts but rather those in the middle of a personality continuum. Academic researchers have given them the name "ambiverts" because (like ambidextrous people who are neither right- nor left-handed) they can glide between extravert and introvert behaviors according to the situation. For their part, introverts are less likely to initiate conversations or want to close deals. Extraverts, on the other hand, can talk too much, listen too little, and contact customers too often (as was the case with my young radio station sales reps). Ambiverts are better able to balance the activities of provocation, inspection, listening, and responding.

There is a bit of a trap to the name, however. Ambidexterity is rare in the general population, but ambiversion is the norm. That is why I call this group the Nimble Majority. You won't find many ambidextrous colleagues around your organization, yet you are very likely surrounded by lots of underutilized members of the Nimble Majority. The natural inclination toward effective customer conversations permeates your organization. Most likely, you are a member of the Nimble Majority yourself.

This line of research confirms my observations of thousands of individuals, and many different types of personalities, represented across functional areas. There are a few unifying characteristics of the people who excel, regardless of exactly where they engage the customer or how much experience they have in doing so.

Think of a champion speed skater. (Even if, like me, you're not a speed skater yourself, then you have likely seen a few minutes of elite speed skating during a Winter Olympics.)

Speed skaters have exceptional acceleration, yet also great balance and a smooth side-to-side motion. They are able to start quickly; good timing makes for an explosive, precise push-off. Champion skaters can also turn on a dime and maneuver through a crowd without getting bladed or stepped upon.

Effective customer conversationalists can likewise start quickly, perhaps with an insightful observation or relevant story. They also adopt a balanced back-and-forth rhythm of speaking and listening. They pay attention to cues from the customer and environment; when necessary, they can speed up or slow down in order to avoid a messy pileup. Because members of the Nimble Majority have enough raw attributes to become adept as messengers, your colleagues don't have to train for thousands of hours to be like an Olympic speed skater. Nor need they wear shiny, skin-tight suits. Thank goodness.

This all means that we should consider not one but three segments of people who can, in different ways, carry your customer conversation: extraverts, Nimble Majority, and introverts. People in these three groups all have a role to play, yet they differ markedly in how they engage with the outside world and where their comfort zones lie.

First, let's discuss your more introverted colleagues. In recent years, there has been a growing recognition of the unique strengths introverts bring to business along with a decreasing professional stigma associated with introversion. Bill Gates, Warren Buffett, and Charles Schwab have all become wildly successful in business despite (or maybe in part because of) being introverted. Still, there are a number of misconceptions about introverts: they're uncomfortable in all social settings, they're particularly afraid of speaking in public, and they gain energy from private reflection. None of these has been shown to be true. Introverts often report as much enjoyment from social settings as do extraverts. With practice and a little desensitization, introverts can not only be good public speakers but also embrace the practice. (David Letterman, George Stephanopoulos, and Malcolm Gladwell are also introverts.) The difference for introverts appears to be in sensitivity to stimulation; prolonged social activity simply means they will need adequate opportunities to recharge.

Extraverts won't be recharging as much as re-stoking. They tend to crave stimulating activities that happen to include social interaction. Perhaps that's another reason why extraverts have traditionally been drawn to sales roles, with their boisterous kickoff meetings and high-octane contests. The challenge in equipping extraverts to be more effective in customer conversations is to get them off the adrenaline rush of near-constant pitching and onto a more balanced approach of listening, selling, and serving.

The majority of your colleagues are, well, in the Nimble Majority. They are perfectly suited for excellence in customer conversations, naturally able to adjust their conversational style to the immediate context. Because of this innate skill, they are less likely to be judged as pushy, insensitive, or arrogant. The challenge is that many people, regardless of personality predispositions, fail to realize how well they and others are equipped for the task. They have been held back—or have held themselves back—due to false assumptions. Bosses, you don't even have to buy your teams sport coats.

THE OPPORTUNITY IS EXPONENTIAL

Chances are, your organization has hamstrung itself to some degree over time. Restricted by assumptions regarding extraversion—needlessly, as we now know—companies have limited both the types and numbers of people whom they entrust with customer relationships. That is a waste of human talent and professional opportunity.

This is much bigger than sales, by the way. It applies to everyone who is engaging (or should be engaging) the outside world in ways that can stimulate business growth, build customer loyalty, and fortify customer relationships. It is about the inherent fitness that you and your colleagues have for transforming the hundreds of customer conversations already taking place every day. And it most certainly includes the people who work in the so-called "back office" and don't have regular customer interaction in their formal job descriptions.

Considering the growth of social media and networking, it's more important than ever to leverage all of your colleagues. Everyone has ties to community leaders, friends in complementary businesses, influencers, and/or friends who represent one or more target buyers for your company's offerings. No one has to necessarily be highly visible or a product expert in order to be an effective contributor to customer conversations. There is a role for everyone, whether it be in planning, creating, and/or delivering your messages. To some degree, everyone close to you and your organization is an expert.

Let's do a little math. The median number of Facebook friends is nearly 200. If you add in other social media channels like LinkedIn, Instagram, and Pinterest, the number of active connections that everyone (front office and back office included) has gets much higher. Yet that's only part of the conversational opportunity. Consider the everyday "analog" conversations that people have around their neighborhoods, tailgate parties, dinner parties, volunteer events, houses of worship, schools, practices, and the like. That likely translates into hundreds of people and thousands of conversational opportunities in a typical month *per person*. Depending on what they say (or don't say), those outside of the organization are forming their opinions of what it is like to buy from you, work for you, donate to you, volunteer for you, or engage with you in the community.

There is a place for everyone, whatever their role in the organization or personality type. For example, introverts can be great informants for creating messages and talking points; they will be attuned to customers' concerns and the nuances of different conversational settings. The extraverts will tend to excel at modeling good conversations, doing role-plays, and generally building confidence across the organization. The Nimble Majority types might be best at showing good practices at community events, networking opportunities, and trade shows, where the interplay between assertive statements and empathetic listening is particularly important.

Similarly, you might prioritize according to conversational opportunities. Who has the most frequent customer contact, and at which point(s) in the customer's decision-making processes? What are the conversation points that can best drive the business? Where are conversations not happening, or happening in a less-than-ideal way? You should allocate people and resources (such as training and incentives) to those conversational opportunities where you can gain near-term traction. You might be missing customer-retention goals because the sales and service teams are having very different interactions with customers. You might be able to cross-sell or up-sell more effectively if the account or operations teams who spend the most time with customers knew which questions to ask. You might generate new opportunities if those delivering or installing your stuff were more confident in answering customers' questions.

Remember that everyone has a role. The introverts might not become six-figure speakers like Malcolm Gladwell, but their innate ability to understand context is valuable to everyone. The extraverts might need a little tamping down, yet their drive to engage the world outside of your organization can motivate others. Their energy is contagious. The Nimble Majority should be unleashed. Their natural flexibility when it comes to listening and speaking provides the model for productive customer conversations. Although we can admire the extraverts' damn-the-torpedoes focus, there is something to be said for taking the torpedoes into account.

GOOD CONVERSATIONS HELP EVERYONE

The transformation of customer conversations is no gimmick, and it is more than a short-term campaign designed to boost sales or employee engagement. Rather, it is a way to share your value with more people in an authentic way (because it is delivered by people who know you best, warts and all). That helps everyone.

Let's consider the difference for consumers when other human beings are involved in their buying process. Just to keep it real, I selected an example that involved two studies and thousands of actual purchases of pizza and booze.

A research team led by Avi Goldfarb compared online orders (which customers submitted on their own) to phone orders (which involved talking to someone else) at a pizza chain during a four-year period. The online orders had, on average, 14 percent more special instructions (such as combining or dividing toppings). The online orders also contained about 100 more calories than did the phone orders. The team also studied sales at fourteen liquor stores in Sweden during a multiyear period, after those stores had introduced a self-service option. In this instance they were looking for any differences in purchases of products whose names were difficult to pronounce. The hypothesis was that people who might be interested in those products would have less fear of embarrassment when trying to say the name to another human being. The result? Market share of the products that were hardest to pronounce increased by more than 8 percent when the stores changed to self-service. The conclusion from these two studies was that buyers behave differently when they aren't sure what to do and/or might be embarrassed in the process. That means that the people in your organization can play a role in leading, informing, motivating, reassuring, and otherwise helping customers in making decisions they won't regret.

You and your teams can improve the buying process—and its outcomes—in several ways. First, they can share what similar customers are doing, and why. One of the most powerful forces shaping human behavior is that of social comparison—our innate anxiety about how we compare to relevant others. Arm your teams with information about the products and services that are most popular, along with who is buying. You can also recommend products and services that go together (maybe pairings of pizza and liquor?). One friend who owns a liquor store makes it a point to help his customers match wines and beers for an event to the foods being served—and at times will share ideas for how to serve and store, too. You can inform buyers of the factors that lead to more satisfaction (or, stated differently, less regret) from buyers. For example, if the vast majority of your customers who buy service contracts are satisfied, that's a useful data point. You can also help buyers wade through the many options (often, too many) available in terms of feature sets, ways of paying, and return/exchange policies. Any of these human interventions will help customers and prospects. And they will happen more frequently and consistently when your organization engages and equips more messengers.

The messengers are better off as well. If you're the leader, the process I describe can break down internal barriers and blind spots—between marketing and sales, or headquarters and field offices, or between the front lines and the back office. It also engages and empowers more individuals, bringing them closer to customers and the great results your organization offers.

THE SHARING GENERATION AWAITS YOUR MESSAGE

During my university professor days, educators would get an annual reminder about how the incoming class would not understand our increasingly dated jokes and cultural references. (We used to joke "The students get younger every year.")

For more than a decade, as fall approaches two faculty members at Beloit College (Ron Neif and Tom McBride) have released the Beloit College Mindset List. It is an unscientific but interesting look at the worldview of incoming college freshmen. They made a number of observations about the Class of 2017 (most of whom were born in or around 1995). During the lifetimes of this new class, spray paint has never legally been sold in Chicago, plasma has never been just a bodily fluid, planes have never landed at Stapleton Airport in Denver, and having a "chat" has seldom involved talking.

This topic is more than an annual conversation starter for teachers, administrators, and parents. Any business that needs to keep its offerings and messages relevant to the next generation must continually adjust its expectations and, ultimately, its marketing approach.

Professors Neif and McBride say this year's group is part of a new and growing "Sharing Generation"—and I tend to agree. They point out a number of ways this manifests itself:

- **Sharing information.** Theirs is a world that has always been marked by cut-and-paste, forward, post, and retweet. The lines between creation and curation (and even plagiarism) are increasingly blurred.

- **Sharing themselves.** Whereas previous generations might recoil at instances of Too Much Information, this generation is texting and "chatting" (in a virtual way) almost all the time and often about personal matters. Of course, some are beginning to understand the potential dangers inherent in sexting or inappropriate Facebook posts.

- **Sharing transportation.** They are tending to flock toward cities and urban centers, have less interest in owning their own vehicles, and are just fine with public transportation.

- **Sharing knowledge.** This group has been exposed to more collaborative learning methods and prefers them. My experience with corporate training and coaching has been similar; most adults want less of a lecture (the "sage on the stage") and more of an expert facilitator (the "guide on the side").

- **A shared national identity.** They've grown up in a multi-ethnic society where diversity and tolerance have been touted throughout their lifetimes. For most, there are many ways to be "American." And no, they don't know much about American history.

- **Shared spiritual values.** This is a generation that often embraces spiritual concepts (meditation, service to others) but not necessarily religious ones. The authors of the Mindset List say today's students are more ecumenical than sectarian. In fact, they assert, this generation may become both the most secular and service-oriented one in American history.

This new mindset, driven by constant connectedness through technology and the erosion of some traditional social structures and norms, has wide implications for all businesses. What is the role of consumer memory when you can look almost anything up? How are community and relationships being reshaped, and will they prove durable for this generation? Marketing messages, networking, and recruiting are continuing to evolve.

Despite the exponential nature of the opportunities in front of them, some organizational leaders get nervous at the prospect of turning their carefully constructed message to (in their view) the masses. They know how, in a digital and viral world, things can go wrong in a hurry if the message is wrong, insensitive, or even just clumsy. In response, they might try to exert an ever-tighter grip on the message and who is allowed to do the talking. So, next we will address the five primary ways that I have seen organizations "mangle" their marketplace messages. These mistakes are often cringe-worthy and costly—but also avoidable. By recognizing the ways that a well-intended message could go awry and adjusting accordingly, leaders can avoid the downside and get to the upside.

Any "Herbs" on your team can come along for the ride, too.

TAKE A MANAGER MOMENT . . .

- Consider the titles and roles across your organization. Where do those colleagues best fit, naturally, into your customer experience? Who is interacting with customers?

- Use those insights to begin your list of highest-potential internal messengers. (In subsequent chapters, you will see ideas for equipping and encouraging them.)

- Now consider messengers on the outside. Which customers, clients, or members are your most enthusiastic fans? Are they well connected? How do they talk about you today?

6

SOMETIMES, THE MESSENGER DOES GET SHOT—
and Deserves It

HAVE YOU EVER HEARD the phrase "Don't shoot the messenger?" At one time, that was a literal admonition.

For centuries across medieval England, the position of town crier was critical. Because most townspeople could not read, the town crier was the singular source of news. Ringing a large hand bell and bellowing "Oyez," the town crier would announce the latest news and proclamations. He typically had other roles too—including the authority to arrest people and take them to the stocks for punishment.

Town criers often had to proclaim—loudly—bad news such as tax increases, so they were protected by law; harming the town crier was considered an act of treason.

These days, there is no such monopoly. Everyone is at some point a messenger. We all tend to worry about the downside of either delivering bad news or delivering news badly. I call these instances "mangled messages." Because there is no King or Queen to save us, those mangled messages can cost businesses dearly in the form of reputation, brand value, and sometimes a whole lot of cash.

MESSAGE MISTAKES HAPPEN. WOW, DO THEY HAPPEN.

Nike is widely recognized as one of the great corporate marketers in business history. They are regularly listed among *Fortune* magazine's "Most Admired Companies." Yet even Nike executives are susceptible to a massive, expensive, and easily avoidable message blunder. As ESPN reported at the time the result allowed Under Armour, then an upstart competitor, to pull off one of the most amazing and valuable marketing switcheroos in history.

Steph Curry has been a unanimous Most Valuable Player in the NBA. He is the league's best shooter and probably its most popular player as well. Curry is not a physically dominant player like LeBron James, nor was he a can't-miss prospect as a young man. He played at Davidson College after the college basketball powerhouses passed on recruiting him. He made a name for himself at Davidson, began his NBA career in the 2009–10 season, and started his first All-Star Game four years later. It took a few years for Curry to ascend the basketball ladder.

The real money for pro basketball players comes in shoe deals and other endorsements. Nike is the dominant force; it has signed more than two-thirds of current NBA players. Curry had been on the Nike roster during his early years in the league (his godfather even worked for Nike), so by 2013 the expectation was that he would extend his relationship. He was, however, willing to listen to Under Armour—new to the shoe game—and the prospect of being that brand's marquee name.

The stakes can be enormous, even beyond a star's playing days. According to *Forbes*, Michael Jordan still makes more than $100 million from Nike each year. He made less than that (nearly $94 million) in total from NBA contracts during his 15-season playing career.

The initial pitch meeting from Nike included several Nike executives along with Steph Curry's father Dell (himself a former NBA player). One Nike official stumbled early in the meeting by mispronouncing Curry's first name. According to ESPN, things only got worse: "A PowerPoint slide featured Kevin Durant's name, presumably left on by accident, presumably residue from repurposed materials." (In case you didn't know, Kevin Durant is another NBA superstar.) The elder Curry told ESPN, "I stopped paying attention after that."

Thanks in large part to Nike's mangled pitch, Under Armour gained the inside track. Curry signed with Under Armour in 2013, and the business marriage has been a raging marketing and financial success. Less than three years later, a Morgan Stanley analyst estimated Curry's potential long-term worth to Under Armour at more than $14 billion. Consider that a measure of the potential power of one conversation.

RECOGNIZE THE MANGLED MESSAGE— AND HOW TO PREVENT IT

Your typical marketplace might not be worth billions. Nevertheless, it's important. You can reap the benefits of a great message, and minimize the impact of a goof-up, by simply recognizing the ways your message could get away from you.

We see cringe-worthy examples nearly every day, along with their marketplace consequences. I use the term "mangled messages" to describe this large category of well-intended but ultimately botched communications. After studying mangled messages over the years, I began to see patterns in the ways that messages go wrong. Here are my top five marks of a mangled message, in no particular order.

Mark of a Mangled Message 1: Not Authentic or Believable

When your audience can fact-check messages with the swipe of a finger across a smartphone screen, you need to get things right. Consider the example of Bruce Braley, an Iowa Democrat who served in the U.S. House of Representatives from 2007 until his defeat in a 2014 U.S. Senate race. Part of his political undoing was the perception among farmers and agricultural interests (a very important group in Iowa, as you might assume) that he did not appreciate them. Braley showed an unfortunate lack of authenticity when he posted to his Facebook page a photo of a farm. It appeared a lovely farm. One would reasonably assume that the picture of a farm on an Iowan's Facebook page would be from Iowa—or at least somewhere in the United States. Some intrepid Facebook users noted that the photo was also listed on *TripAdvisor.com* as the Cammas Hall Fruit Farm in England. Braley's team removed the post but the damage had been done. Voters didn't appreciate the gaffe, and the aspiring Senator's campaign "bought the farm."

You might say, "Jim, highlighting the missteps of truth-challenged politicians and their campaigns as mangled messages is just too easy." You would have a point. How about another example—set in Washington, DC but not involving a politician?

The scene was a July evening. Across America, millions of TV viewers were watching the annual PBS live special "A Capitol Fourth"—which includes the huge Independence Day fireworks show over the Capitol's West Lawn. Onscreen were brilliant fireworks bursting against a clear sky, even though it was cloudy in Washington, DC that night. There was another clue that something was amiss: some footage of the supposedly live fireworks showed the Capitol dome without any scaffolding. At that moment, the Capitol building was undergoing significant renovations. Many viewers took notice. A representative tweet, from @kdittmar, read: *Not only did they clear the clouds out of the sky, #July4thPBS cleared the scaffolding off of the Capitol.*

What was going on? In order to make the fireworks display look better for television, PBS officials decided to mix footage from prior years with the live broadcast. They also decided not to tell anyone. Later, PBS confirmed that the supposedly live show was not actually live—but their message was dismissive. The show's Twitter feed read, "We showed a combination of the best fireworks from this year and previous years. It was the patriotic thing to do."

What in the name of Francis Scott Key does a lack of authenticity have to do with patriotism?

The lesson: Never try to sneak something past your audience—especially when the truth is, well, self-evident.

Mark of a Mangled Message #2: Detached from Reality

Good customer messages are largely focused on the customers—their needs, desires, hopes, and challenges. When the message fails to recognize the realities of the customer's world, companies unwittingly create friction in the relationship. Have you ever received a message and thought, "Which world do these people live in?"

Not long ago, my wife and I decided to add a swimming pool to the family home. (This is the "dig a large hole in your backyard and pour in the money" strategy. I'm not sure that I recommend it.) Buying a pool ultimately involves buying a lot more than just the pool. One of those apparently necessary items is a set of lounge chairs; we selected a set from a high-end catalog retailer. They arrived flat-packed, ready to assemble. In each box were furniture pieces, a package of hardware (bolts, washers, wheels), and a set of instructions. These so-called instructions contained no actual words, no indication of sequence, and woefully inadequate illustrations. At least it was a simple task—even yours truly could figure it out—and I wasn't under great time pressure. Imagine if you were trying to assemble a tricycle on Christmas Eve with lousy instructions!

This particular instruction sheet was completely detached from the reality of the person who ultimately depends on that information. It implicitly says, "I'm not thinking about you, the customer. I care about shipping product out my door and not so much about what happens when it gets to your door." With minimal effort—a customer panel, perhaps a little research with users—the customer experience could have been vastly improved.

Big brand names often demonstrate the same unfortunate detachment. Three of the world's largest airlines had similarly tone-deaf advertising campaigns out at the same time. American Airlines introduced ads touting "The World's Greatest Flyers"—passengers who, among other things, "walk faster in airports than anywhere else." Your experience might be different, but when I speed-walk (or jog) through an airport, it's typically because my connecting flight was late. The airline typically bears some responsibility. Please, airline, don't congratulate customers for dealing with messes that you helped create!

For their part, other airlines have shown glimpses of cluenessless as well. Delta Airlines introduced a campaign titled "Keep Climbing" (which begs the question: climbing higher than what? The industry has a dreadful customer-satisfaction track record). United dusted off a decades-old tagline of "The Friendly Skies," which it originally introduced when Eastern, TWA, and Pan Am shared the skies and air travel was a friendlier experience. Nostalgia is not the same as reality. Few airlines appear to understand the reality of their own customers today.

Mark of a Mangled Message #3: Focused on the Sender, Not the Receiver

As discussed in Chapter 3, we are naturally and chemically inclined to talk about ourselves and what we know best. That means in business conversations we tend to focus on our company, our brand, and the products or services we offer. Unfortunately, that can unwittingly make us sound like the boor who sits next to you on an airplane and launches into his life story—overwhelming the opportunity for a mutually valuable conversation.

The major hotel chains are, in at least one messaging setting, consistent manglers. If you have stayed in a hotel lately, then you likely have noticed a message asking you to reuse towels and linens. Sometimes there is an accompanying offer of a discount or bonus loyalty points. When guests switch towels and linens less often, there can be benefits all the way around—to the guest (bonus goodies), to the hotel (lower costs), and to the environment (less impact). For the most part, these programs are successful; according to industry reports, most guests given the opportunity do indeed reuse towels at least once during their stay. Yet, a more receiver-focused message would likely produce even better results.

The hotel chain that gets most of my business has an in-room card that reads, "As we care for you, we care for our planet." Hmmm. That message mentions the hotel and the planet, but not the guest! Interestingly enough, research is pretty clear that a message of social proof—illustrating to the guest what other guests are doing—is most effective. In a controlled study, when guests were told that most others in the hotel reused their towels, they became 26 percent more likely to reuse their towels. You want to be more specific? When guests were told that most others who stayed *in their particular room* reused their towels, then they became 33 percent more likely.

Nowhere in the research is there a "we care" message. I have been a guest in all of the major hotel chains; they each tend to have a similar theme. How much more value could they produce with a more customer-focused message?

Mark of a Mangled Message #4: Delivered Inconsistently

You might have a compelling message—but if it looks and sounds different across settings then it likely won't resonate. It will feel false.

For months, my local dry cleaner had a sign on the counter that read "Having fun while we're getting it done!" (along with a plea to like them on Facebook). The message bore little resemblance to my usual customer experience, which was fine but not fun; most of the young employees at the counter go through the motions while the crew in the back is normally silent and focused (and sometimes sweaty). That's okay, because as a customer I care more about my "getting it done" reality than their "having fun" veneer.

After a few months, I noticed that the sign had been removed. When I asked one of the employees about it, she rolled her eyes and said, "Yeah, we used to laugh about that here. No one cared."

My dry cleaner was tossing out a relatively banal, one-off message that was disconnected from the other things they wanted customers to believe about them. No real harm was done. But some big retailers have managed over the years to spread messages so fundamentally inconsistent that the brand itself became damaged goods.

At one time Radio Shack was a fixture across the United States, with thousands of stores offering nearly everything related to electronics. It was the place to go, especially for hobbyists and those looking for cables, replacement parts, and the stuff to make gadgets go. In the 1990s, at its peak, the company launched a big advertising campaign with the tagline, "You've got questions, we've got answers." It turned out to be a setup; that promise made through the media was nothing like the in-person messages that many customers got at the stores. As one customer posted on a message board at the time: "Trust me, they do not have answers. Just your phone number and address. What do you expect from someone making less than the kid at McDonald's?"

Radio Shack eventually descended into bankruptcy. That slogan—and the inconsistency it produced—lives on as a punchline.

Mark of a Mangled Message #5: Not Conveyed Skillfully

Sometimes a seemingly well-intentioned idea gets mangled because the messenger lacks skill with the right words or visuals. Or, they might be oblivious to larger themes.

For those of us who appreciate the significance of the 9/11 attacks in 2001, for example, each anniversary is a solemn remembrance. For others, unfortunately, it is just another promotional opportunity. On one particular anniversary a lingerie marketer tweeted, *"Rembering (sic) those who lost their lives on September 11, 2001. 40% OFF*

END OF SUMMER CLEARANCE." Is a sober, thoughtful remembrance (or even rembrance) of a human tragedy really consistent with a clearance sale on lingerie? Who writes this stuff?

Twitter and other social media platforms are full of boneheaded, poorly executed messages. That should not be a surprise given that basic communication skills are in chronically short supply. You and I can't tackle the issues in skill development for working professionals, but we can look at these unfortunate cases in the name of our own education. How convenient it is, then, that a legitimately fine educational institution demonstrated an avoidable mangled message.

Drake University, located in Des Moines, has built a reputation in the liberal arts. Several of Drake's professional programs, such as its law school, are also highly ranked nationally.

The university's leadership commissioned a new recruitment campaign, a collaboration among its Admissions office, its Marketing and Communications staff, and an outside agency. The team hoped that its campaign would prove interesting to attention-challenged teens. Following months of research and creative development, the new campaign debuted with this theme: "Drake = D+."

Get it? "D" is for Drake, and the plus is for all of the benefits that occur when Drake and a student get together. A large "D+" dominated the new recruitment materials.

Of course, when it comes to education a "D+" has another connotation: a poor grade. Either the folks at Drake somehow did not consider this or they let their agency advisers talk them into something. Faculty, staff members, alumni, and other constituencies were not amused. Apparently Drake failed to involve them in designing or testing the campaign. An internal email to faculty and staff, crafted to defuse criticism, included this: "In our eagerness to launch Drake Advantage . . . we neglected to invite faculty and staff to preview the campaign . . . we are very sorry that many of you were caught by surprise as a result."

The only market research mentioned in that email was an online survey of high school students. The kids had been asked, for example, whether the concept would get their attention and whether it differentiated Drake from other universities. So, because a narrow group of survey respondents found the concept to be distinctive and attention-grabbing Drake went ahead with the launch. (Setting oneself on fire is both distinctive and attention-grabbing as well, but it also produces a low-quality state of affairs.) A better route would have considered the views of alumni, faculty, and staff members so that the finished product would make all of Drake's core constituencies proud. I suspect that, during the time message ideas were being bandied about, some alumnus, professor, or staff member would have pointed out the problem with "D+" before any damage could occur.

SOMETIMES THERE IS AUDIENCE MALICE

These examples have something in common: they represent some sort of unforced error. Each to some degree was sloppy, incomplete, self-focused, false, and/or misleading. But these days, the very nature of digital communication assets means that a message can also get hijacked and deliberately taken out of context. This adds a new element of vulnerability.

The consumer goods giant Unilever has experienced this phenomenon. The company has had great success over the years with its "Campaign for Real Beauty" for Dove soap.

Creatives and critics alike have consistently applauded the campaign's bold, counterintuitive, and timely point of view. Industry judges for *Advertising Age* rated it at the very top of 21st Century Ad Campaigns.

The campaign has been deliberately provocative, prompting conversations about standards of beauty and female self-esteem. On one occasion Dove was posting a brief online video ad on Facebook. The full clip showed an African American woman morphing into a White woman who then transitions to another woman of color. But someone in the digital audience made a frame grab, depicting only that first change (the African American woman taking off a t-shirt to reveal a White woman underneath). The frame grab went viral. That smaller chunk taken out of a longer story had a far different meaning to some, who interpreted the message as racist.

The Unilever experience illustrates that today others can actively edit your own message to work against you. These days, we have to consider how the message might get snipped, shared, and removed from its original context.

In the legendary (at least to me) 1980 comedy film *Used Cars*, a conniving competitor to the heroes' used-car lot managed to sneak an edit of their local TV ad. In the original ad, the naïve and well-intentioned owner said they had "styles of cars to choose from" and that her lot was "one mile west" of a certain route. The dirty-trick edit was made so that she appeared to claim they had "miles of cars." The conniving competitor sued for false advertising. In the movie, the heroes had to secure enough inventory to prove to a judge that there was in fact more than a mile of cars on the lot.

Part of the comedy was the absurdity of the rough, obvious edit. Today it is relatively easy to edit others' content to substantially change its meaning. Your competition, the disgruntled, the clueless, and haters everywhere, can all mess with your message. How can a well-intentioned professional cope?

THE TENDENCY IS TO TIGHTEN, OR TURN COAL INTO DIAMONDS

Your business message, in all its forms, is a tremendous daily opportunity for growth. Unfortunately, it also leaves you exposed—to internal mistakes and oversights as well as to external malcontents. How should one balance the substantial and consistent upside versus the occasional downside?

Some executives tighten up. To borrow a slightly expurgated line from the classic (again, at least to me) movie *Ferris Bueller's Day Off:* "*The boy cannot relax. Pardon my French, but Cameron is so tight that if you stuck a lump of coal up his a**, in two weeks you'd have a diamond.*"

What do the Camerons of the business world do? Some will take a pass on saying anything at all. They will fail to equip their people with the language or tools they need— and in the process leave all of those growth opportunities to the competition. Others will decide to put a message out there—one so bland and risk-averse that it forms no signal at all. Their organizations just blend into the environmental noise. Some will be overly secretive in developing the message, as if the team were guarding something as vital as nuclear codes . . . or even the Coca-Cola formula.

That would be a shame if it happened to your organization. The point of diving into these various mangled messages is to better understand how companies and professionals of varying stripes can take advantage of their opportunities while avoiding common mistakes. We can learn a great deal about a concept by studying its opposite.

This might seem counterintuitive, but often the organizations that work hardest to avoid mistakes set themselves up to commit them. I find it best to resolve, as a team, to take advantage of the growth opportunities hiding in plain sight. Then make it an organizational effort! If by chance there is a major slip-up, then there will be a lot of people ready to help set things straight right away.

HOW TO RESPOND IF YOUR MESSAGE GETS MANGLED ANYWAY

Mistakes can and do happen. On occasion, as was the case with Unilever and Dove, you might not have even done much of anything wrong yourself; competitors or busybodies will deliberately misstate or misrepresent things.

In such cases, communication experts generally agree on the best practices to follow. For example, the Plank Center for Leadership in Public Relations at the University of Alabama offers these guidelines for responding to a communications crisis:

- Have a plan before things go wrong. You can use the exercise at the end of this chapter to get started.

- Rehearse. This is a bit like a fire drill. No one should have to think about the plan (or, worse, find it) during the moment of crisis.

- Respond quickly. Nature doesn't tolerate a vacuum. Neither does a crisis. In the absence of your response the marketplace will make its own (mostly inaccurate) assumptions about the facts and your motivations.

- Choose one person who will act as the messenger. These are the times when an organization needs one voice of authority and empathy. Choose strategically. You'll want someone with adequate knowledge, skill, and confidence for the role.

- Stay truthful and consistent. I advise clients to stay away from hypotheticals; don't comment on things you do not know about. If you don't have all the answers, simply say so but come back to your audiences as soon as you can.

- Be direct, not evasive. "No comment" actually is a message and it isn't the one you want to convey.

- Have a dedicated web page to deal with the crisis. It is a great idea to have a template set up and inactive. You can then quickly link that page to all social media sites.

- Show your empathy for anyone who has been harmed or inconvenienced. Giving voice to your concern is not an admission of guilt, but rather a human thing to do. Time and again we see executives, coaches, entertainers, or others in the limelight offer what I call "the non-apology apology." They will say such drivel as "If you felt let down then we are sorry," "We are sorry about the situation," or "It is an unfortunate incident, one that we all can learn from."

- When things have subsided, it's time to evaluate all of the activities. And remember to debrief the crisis team, recognize contributions, and update the plan if needed.

These message problems, although sometimes embarrassing, are rarely fatal for the business. Sometimes your relationships with customers, employees, and communities actually emerge stronger. Don't allow any anxiety to hold you back.

Your business likely has many messengers-in-waiting. Next, let's talk about some ways you can help make them most effective.

TAKE A MANAGER MOMENT . . .

- Consider each of the five marks of a mangled message. Rate your vulnerability to each (either on a numeric scale or just low/moderate/high) and have some colleagues do likewise. Is the leadership team in general agreement?

- What are you doing to guard against potential messaging slip-ups? Who has visibility and accountability?

- If you don't yet have a contingency plan for dealing with a major communication crisis, then start right away. Assign roles, put the plan in writing, and practice before you would ever need to go into action.

7

NOT EVERY MESSENGER
IS CREATED EQUAL
(But Nearly All Can Be Effective)

"THE BOSS SAID TO CHANGE the sign, so I did."

I once saw this message on the marquee outside of a local retailer. Actually, I have seen this same message many times over the years on the marquees of other retailers, fast-food restaurants, and convenience stores. It seemed clever the first time. Now I recognize such messages as wasted opportunities, considering the fact that thousands of drivers and passengers go by these businesses each day.

One Saturday afternoon, while performing my various husband and dad errands, I kept track of the content in the marquees I drove by (in a safe manner, of course). Here was my count:

- Seventeen businesses used their signs to announce sales. Quite reasonable.

- Four businesses had a message about a new product. Ditto.

- Two marquees, situated directly under signs featuring the name of the business, simply repeated the name of the business. Not incrementally helpful.

- Two businesses used their marquees to announce "Help Wanted."

- Three businesses used the marquee to offer non-sales messages (think brief, motivational slogans).

- One marquee had only "Closed."

- Four businesses had absolutely nothing on their marquees.

Think about all of the people who have a connection to your business and an interest in seeing it (and you) succeed. Depending on your type of business, these may be employees, contract workers, customers, suppliers, distributors, officials, alumni, members, donors, volunteers, community leaders, and friends. Together they represent hundreds—or even thousands—of "marquees" for you as they go about their everyday interactions. Unfortunately, in my experience the majority of potential messengers for most businesses are a blank sign. They are neither equipped with the knowledge of how they could help nor activated to actually do so.

When you look at the totality of your business relationships, do you suspect many of them represent blank, bland, or disconnected marquees? If so, the crickets might be chirping unnecessarily. You have an enormous opportunity to engage lots of these individuals as messengers for growth. You need not be pushy, creepy, or sales-y.

Your relationships are not some monolith, on standby to be programmed and dispatched. They are, of course, a set of individuals with important variations. Some might be longtime friends; you have known each other but never cross paths professionally. Others might be more recent or transactional. Across the board, they likely are a combination of different demographic categories, communication preferences, experiences, and status.

No single script, program, or enticement is going to work with all of them. (That would be an insult anyway!) But those differences are less important in practice than are the similarities.

You saw in Chapter 5 the evidence that, by personality, most of us are naturally wired for these conversations. In this chapter, we will put common assumptions about generational differences under the microscope as well. Spoiler alert: It turns out that professionals across the age spectrum value and use face-to-face conversation to remarkably similar degrees. I have also found that—for nearly everyone—our effectiveness as messengers mostly comes down to three factors that have little if anything to do with demographics.

IS THERE A GENERATION GAP IN COMMUNICATION?

The principles in this book are valuable for professionals across age and cultural categories. Even so, we need to take stock of the major demographic trends affecting workplaces everywhere.

In the United States, the so-called Millennial generation (generally defined as those born between 1981 and 1996) is the largest segment in the workforce. Millennials now outnumber the Generation X and Baby Boomer segments in terms of the numbers of those either working or looking for work. Close on their heels are the post-Millennial (Generation Y) age group, the oldest of whom are now workers too.

I tend to discount the value of wide, clunky categories such as "Millennials" or "Boomers" when it comes to explaining human behavior. However, when it comes to the relationships that professionals have with technology and communication, well, we should recognize the obvious. Technological changes have come at us rapidly. We can expect different communication styles, expectations, and comfort levels based on age categories and experiences.

The Baby Boomers have spent much of their lives immersed in face-to-face and phone conversations before bringing the digital world (at least some elements of it) into their lives. Generation Y is generally regarded as the first digital-native generation. Generation X and the Millennials represent a progression along the continuum. The digital communication world is inherently efficient and scalable. It is also on the sterile side, lacking the intimacy and nonverbal elements of more personal and face-to-face communication. Where is the younger professional set landing?

Wei Lui's research into Generation Y reveals a few characteristics of their preferred communication styles, namely that it be

- Instant (immediate and spontaneous)
- Playful (enjoyable and challenging)
- Collaborative (supportive, unifying, and shared)
- Expressive (open, free, and animated)
- Responsive (alert and quick)
- Flexible (adaptable and accommodating)

What isn't completely clear is how different these preferences are from those of other generations. In fact, some survey research shows that the younger set has some fairly old-school ideas about communication and technology. For example, a study from the HR services firm Randstad showed that most members of Generations Y and Z preferred face-to-face communication with managers over emails or instant messaging. Only 14 percent believed that technology improves personal relationships with co-workers.

Yes, there will be natural variations among employees, colleagues, customers, and everyone else who can serve as messengers. But when it comes to managing your message, let's not make this more complicated than it needs to be. There are important similarities and unifying factors across the generational spectrum. A few factors will tend to determine the success of your messengers, regardless of whether they are long in the tooth, cutting their teeth, or somewhere in between.

THE THREE THINGS YOUR FUTURE MESSENGERS NEED MOST

Think of the people you consider to already be great advocates and messengers. They might be employees, partners, or maybe a customer. What is it about them that makes them so compelling and effective?

Over the years, I found that great messengers had certain qualities. They have something specific to say (typically, an experience they want to share). They are comfortable in the way they express themselves, whether their medium of choice is face-to-face conversation, social media, or something else. They are also proactive about sharing what they know with people they believe will benefit from it.

Putting on the professor and consultant hats, I have come to see these three high-level characteristics of effective messengers as

* Knowledge
* Skill
* Confidence

If that is what the conversation is like when someone has all three elements, what happens when one of the elements is absent? How do we know when a messenger could use our help in a particular area?

If messengers lack knowledge about a particular organization, they will likely make poor recommendations. It's not that they would intend to. But if your knowledge of a company's products, services, or values is incomplete or dated, you lack the basic data to talk about it or recommend it to others.

If communication skill is missing, the audience will likely be distracted. It is simply difficult to get past obvious problems with word choice, grammar, or stories; the audience tends to focus on the communication misstep much like they might "rubberneck" to notice a fender-bender accident on the road to work. As noted in Chapter 6, the lack of skill can lead to a mangled message.

If confidence is low, there is unrealized value—for both the potential messenger and the people he or she can help. Such messengers don't engage and don't offer the world the benefits of their experience and training. It's a shame, because as we have seen most people are naturally wired for competence in conversation.

Let's equip more messengers with what they need so that they will engage, making their recommendations and sharing their ideas in ways that get the right type of attention.

KNOWLEDGE: WHAT DOES EVERYONE NEED TO KNOW?

I once heard the CEO of a fast-casual restaurant chain report that, when she first took on her leadership role, "More people knew how to apply for time off than knew what was on our menu."

For restaurants, the menu is a literal asset; it sets out all of the things that the restaurant offers to customers. For non-restaurant businesses, your menu is a more symbolic concept. But let's get real here. Do your employees know all of the things that customers can buy from you? Do they understand what your best customers are like and *why* they choose to buy from you?

This is not a pop quiz, of course. No one expects encyclopedic knowledge. We do, however, want people to have relevant knowledge rooted in the specifics of their most common customer interactions.

Alex Goldfayn consults with many companies—typically mid-sized private companies in mature industries—to help them grow sales revenue. Over the years he has asked thousands of business leaders to estimate what Alex calls their "awareness percentage," or the percentage of the total portfolio of products and services that their customers are even aware of. Alex reports an average awareness percentage of only 25 percent. That means customers—who often have been customers for many years—do not know about three-quarters of the things the company sells. That can constrict a business.

Without knowledge of the basics—as you define them for your organization—messengers cannot be prepared to offer perspective, advice, or recommendations. Their default mode will be to give customers too many options. That only makes things more difficult. It's the difference between "You must try this great restaurant!" and "There are lots of options . . . I'm sure you will find one that's good for you."

SKILLS: SAY IT LIKE YOU MEAN IT

It is easy it is to fall into sloppy patterns of speech and other communication forms. Some of those corrosive patterns might be costing you plenty.

Many salespeople, product leaders, and subject matter experts—particularly those in technology companies—are now in the habit of starting sentences with "So." Buyers are starting to notice and typically find it annoying. I have even caught myself doing it a few times lately; I might need the equivalent of a swear jar to head that one off.

If "so" is potentially a bit annoying, another persistent speech habit can be truly damaging. "Upspeaking," the pattern of ending a sentence with a rising pitch (so that a declaration sounds like a question), is itself on the rise. The trend even has a name: high-rising terminal (HRT). The pattern gained a foothold among American teens years ago and has unfortunately followed many of them into adulthood. HRT has also spread across age groups in the United States as well as into other nations and cultures.

Interestingly, HRT has long been the norm in Australia and New Zealand (it's known as the "Australian Question Intonation"). American and Aussie TV shows consumed in the United Kingdom are being blamed for spreading upspeak among professional Brits. A study of British managers and executives from the publishing giant Pearson found that most (71 percent) agree upspeaking is a "particularly annoying trait"; more than 80 percent said it is "a clear indicator of a person's insecurity or emotional weakness." More than half said upspeakers would be limited in job promotions and raises within their organization.

HRT isn't just for Valley Girls anymore, and it obviously damages credibility and persuasiveness.

My observation has been that women use upspeak much more often than do men. A clever study in the journal *Gender & Society* demonstrated the pattern.

If HRT serves to frame statements in the form of a question, the game show *Jeopardy!* would probably be a great laboratory for examining the practice. That's what Tom Linneman did—he examined 100 episodes with 300 contestants and a total of 5,500 responses. On the show, women did indeed use upspeak twice as often as did the male contestants. But another interesting gender difference emerged as well. For the men, the frequency of upspeak changed with success or failure; men who answered correctly used upspeak 27 percent of the time but those who were incorrect used it 57 percent of the time. The female contestants who answered correctly used upspeak 48 percent of the time, and that didn't vary significantly when they were incorrect.

Upspeak is a pervasive and unhealthy communications trend. It will hold you back in a professional setting. Young women are particularly susceptible to using HRT as well as being undermined by it. If you are looking for a professionally limiting habit to shed—or if you are trying to help a work colleague, your child, or a young adult you're mentoring—then addressing HRT might be the place to begin.

So I guess you'll want to get on that?

MORE SKILLS: LEND THE WORLD YOUR EAR

One of the sayings around my Georgia hometown was, "You got two ears and one mouth, so you probably ought to do more listening than talking." In today's professional world, if you ask high performers about their most valuable skills, you are likely to hear something about "listening" near the top of the list. And yet professionals with great expertise can be the worst offenders. We are problem solvers, with fine-tuned radar to locate patterns. We know (or think we know) the path that will be best, and we want to get right to it.

For example, who is more of an expert problem solver than your doctor? We need our doctor's expertise, yet most patient encounters with their doctors don't involve much in the way of listening.

According to a study of actual doctor-patient conversations, physicians give patients an average of just 11 seconds to describe their issue before cutting them off. Specialists are on average even less patient than are general practitioners. Only 20 percent of specialists give patients the opportunity to describe their issue at the onset of a consultation. That is startling. Sure, the specialist might have received some briefing on the patient's problem through a referral or a nurse's report. But as the study's co-author Naykyy Singh Ospina said in an interview, "Even in a specialty visit concerning a specific matter, it is invaluable to understand *why* the patients think they are at the appointment and what specific concerns they have related to the condition or its management."

When the doctor-patient conversation is more interactive, good things happen. Patients even save money. A research team from Duke University's Fuqua School of Business, the Duke University School of Medicine, and several other institutions examined actual recorded dialogue from more than 1,700 outpatient visits. The patients were dealing with breast cancer, depression, or rheumatoid arthritis— all conditions with potentially high out-of-pocket costs. The conversations involved oncologists, psychiatrists, and rheumatologists.

The researchers wanted to learn how often cost came up in the conversation, who brought it up, and what the results were. Among the findings:

- Cost was part of the doctor-patient conversation 30 percent of the time. This was an increase from studies conducted several years prior.

- Doctors were just as likely to bring up the topic of cost as were their patients.

- The cost component of the conversation usually lasted one minute or less.

- In nearly half of those times when cost was discussed, either the doctor or the patient came up with a simple strategy to lower cost.

The most typical areas for cost savings included switching pharmacies, using co-pay assistance or drug coupons, switching to lower-cost tests, and using free samples of new medications. The patients' overall care plans were usually not affected.

If doctors are actually becoming more proactive in their conversations, then it would be a promising trend for all concerned. The very notion of "improved patient conversations" has seemed like a double-edged sword to many of the physicians with whom I've spoken. Doctors certainly want their patients to see them sooner (before small issues become larger ones), be more forthcoming, and ask questions. At the same time, more patients have come to those conversations already armed with assumptions (often picked up online) and preferences (based on advertising for prescription drugs). Doctors complain that patients pressure them for unnecessary drugs, tests, or procedures—or don't follow their instructions after the visit. In response, medical groups are trying to regain control of the conversation.

There are important lessons here for medical conversations—but also for anyone marketing complex and/or higher-priced products and services. Issues like cost are uncomfortable for potential buyers; they feel vulnerable because they believe they are at an information disadvantage. You might lose a sale just because the potential buyer isn't aware of options and does not want to bring up the topic.

CONFIDENCE: "I CAN DO THIS"

Have you seen someone who appears to have all the knowledge, skills, and incentives necessary to perform well—yet they never "get into it"? It is relatively easy to come up with excuses, put it off, set other priorities, or leave the conversation to someone else.

When it comes to sharing an important message—even one that people believe to be true, valuable, and important—why is it that some will hesitate or avoid altogether?

I once helped to lead a training event for a corporate client, when new messaging (including a conversation designed to be led from a whiteboard) was introduced to approximately a hundred sales and sales-support professionals. Most of the participants had been with the company, or at least in the industry, for many years.

An important element of the training was to have everyone practice the whiteboard conversation with a colleague, after which a couple of people (those who seemed particularly comfortable with it) were asked if they would come to the front of the room and role-play for the entire group. The "winner" according to audience applause would receive a nice prize. On this day the winner was a woman in her twenties. She had been with the company for exactly one day before the training.

It would have been natural and expected for this woman to hang back during the competition. Even when her practice performance stood out, it would have easier to decline the offer rather than get in front of a hundred brand-new colleagues. Where did all of that confidence come from? More importantly, how can we help our potential messengers take what they know and infuse it with enough confidence so that they don't sit on the fence?

We can find some clues in other domains. A study of college athletes, for example, showed that variables such as mastery, demonstration of ability, preparation, and social support were most important in building self-confidence.

When it comes to business messaging, here are the most important confidence-building beliefs that I find in messengers:

- "I can do this." This is the belief that your knowledge and skill levels are adequate for the types of conversations you will be having.

- "I don't have to be perfect." Confident messengers know they won't be called out or punished if something is not quite right. Managers can reinforce this belief by making and keeping the promise that, as long as someone isn't lying, they won't face any sanction for doing their best to spread the message and help others.

- "This feels right to me." Confident messengers believe that the message itself is both authentic and a good fit for how they want the world to see them.

- "I'm not alone." They see their peers and friends doing similar things and have confidence that members of the group will support one another.

WHAT ABOUT YOUR PASSIONATE CORE?

Sometimes there are employees, customers, members, or volunteers for whom confidence doesn't seem to be a problem. They are the ones who jump into the conversational fray without much prompting or encouragement. They tell lots of other people about their experiences. They might even dream about it, for all we know.

These are the passionate fans, and every organization wants them. They bring energy and enthusiasm. Nevertheless, many passionate and well-intentioned people are lousy messengers for the organizations and causes they are most passionate about.

Consider the example of climate change, an ongoing conversation for several decades now worldwide. (I'm not expressing a political opinion on the issue, by the way. Let's just not.) There has been an interesting evolution in both the language of the debate and public opinion over time. Gallup's annual survey about the environment reveals three segments within the US population when it comes to beliefs about climate change: Concerned Believers (nearly half of adults), the Mixed Middle (about one-third), and Cool Skeptics (about one-fifth). Overall opinions have been relatively steady for several years, although the divisions by segment are increasingly defined along partisan lines. Americans have settled into their views about what policies, if any, are necessary for climate protection.

Beyond policy matters, Americans continue to support the idea of care for the environment. A 2017 survey from the Pew Research Center found that 74 percent of US adults agree "the country should do whatever it takes to protect the environment." Fair enough. But then the numbers get really interesting.

Since the late 1980s, Gallup has asked Americans this question: "Do you consider yourself an environmentalist, or not?" In May 1989, a total of 76 percent of their sample responded "yes." In 1995 that still described a majority of Americans but fell to 63 percent. By 1999 the number was down to 50 percent. By 2018 it was 42 percent.

How is it that nearly three-quarters of Americans feel strongly that the environment requires protection, yet fewer than half consider themselves environmentalists? There is no simple answer, but I strongly suspect that the messaging from some of the most passionate environmentalists is part of the issue.

Many climate activists have taken to publicly calling out their opponents as "deniers." Perhaps they are frustrated and want immediate action. Perhaps they are convinced that the weight of evidence is on their side, even though thoughtful and well-intentioned people can raise legitimate questions about measurements of surface temperatures. But the cycle of "No, I'm not!" and "Yes, you are!" won't lead anywhere.

It's important to remember that the best rallying cries are generally framed toward the positive. Heifer International is about "ending hunger and poverty." Ambassadors of Compassion is about "equipping youth for life." Sometimes an effective message is focused on alleviating a negative, as with the Wounded Warrior Project ("the greatest casualty is being forgotten"). In either case, the audience should feel that they can personally affect an improved outcome.

The positive force that brings people into the group can, unfortunately, easily lead to a negative counter force. We know from social psychology that those who identify themselves into a group (for them, the "ingroup") can easily denigrate those on the outside of the group (the "outgroup"). When the messaging loses its focus on the positive outcomes to be achieved and instead descends into comments on an outgroup, the cause itself can get stuck. That's likely contributing to the Gallup results.

Whether your passion is for the environment, a company, your community, education, economic opportunity, or anything else, the clear and positive discipline of your messaging will to a large degree determine your probability of success. The "Mixed Middle" is on the fence, listening to what both sides have to say and evaluating the tribes.

Your base of messengers and potential messengers is likely diverse—cutting across roles, experiences, and age categories. They also have a lot in common. They are looking for connections.

They will also be looking to others for the example to follow. Another spoiler alert: It very well might be the person staring back at you in the mirror.

TAKE A MANAGER MOMENT . . .

- Go back to your list of potential messengers. For each segment, evaluate your status quo.

- What do they know today about your offerings and options? Do they know any great customer stories? Where are they learning these things, formally or informally?

- In general, how do you evaluate their skill levels in communication? Given their strengths and weaknesses, what will be the most natural and comfortable settings for them?

- How are you building conversational confidence, within and across teams?

- Are there any potentially overly enthusiastic messengers who need to be (gently) reined in?

Part Three

A NEW SET OF
MANAGEMENT HABITS

8

YOU CAN BE A
CONVERSATIONAL LEADER
(And Probably Need to Be)

HAVE YOU EVER BEEN "VOLUNTOLD"? This means to be told to do something, under the guise of volunteering. Within many big companies, the term "voluntold" is bandied about freely.

The scenario typically plays out like this. The leadership has announced an important new project or initiative, one that needs expert input from a few people inside the organization. These should ideally be individuals who have been successful in this particular domain, who have distinctive knowledge to tap or skills that others could model, and who have earned a high level of credibility inside the organization.

Where does the project leader find these expert doers? Chances are, they are busy doing. That's what they do.

When I work with larger corporate clients on messaging projects, there is a similar dynamic. The project sponsor—a high-ranking executive responsible for business results—identifies a few key individuals to involve. We try to select a diverse mix, involving people from different business units, locations, and experiences. But it's most important to recruit people who know what they are doing, are generous in helping others, and have "street cred." With professionals like that involved, we can be confident that the work product will be useful and practical—and that our intended users will want to use it.

There is a potential problem, however. Those internal experts aren't sitting around, waiting idly for an invitation to join another project team. They are in the field, meeting with customers, coaching team members, adding to their knowledge base, and otherwise doing the things that make them so valuable in the first place. "Should we take them out of the field, even for just a little while?" some executives worry. It is a fundamental tension that the busiest people most in demand are exactly the ones whose help we need when it comes to building and sharing the message. But it's likewise clear that securing a little time and attention from the so-called A-players will generate many times higher returns than allowing mediocre messaging to drag the organization down, day after month after year.

Besides, in every case the "voluntoldees" have jumped into their projects with good cheer. They understand the value of great messaging and are typically flattered to be asked to participate.

You might be in a different situation. Perhaps you lead a smaller organization or are in a solo business. If that's the case, you are already, by default, the message leader. Even if you are managing yourself rather than a bunch of direct reports, you have to consider all of those potential messengers on the outside—your current clients or customers, suppliers, partners, members, donors, and friends. The lessons here still apply, regardless of the organizational chart (if one even exists).

Tag, you're it.

ISN'T THIS THE CEO'S JOB?

We might naturally think that the overall organizational leader should also assume the role of messaging leader. After all, who has more contact with all the constituencies of a business—and who else is the primary keeper of the mission? The top boss might have all of the personal characteristics and experience to be a great messaging leader in theory, yet lack the visibility or perspective necessary to make the message hum in practice.

Researchers Michael Porter and Nitin Nohria had an interesting idea. They wanted to know how CEOs actually spent their time. They found 27 CEOs of large, global firms who agreed to share their schedules. The CEOs' executive assistants did the actual recording, in 15-minute increments, over periods of several weeks.

As you might suspect, these big-company CEOs work a lot and they are "always on." The leaders in the study worked nearly ten hours per weekday, about four hours daily on the weekends, and more than two hours per day on vacations. About half of that work was done at company headquarters; the remainder included time spent at other company locations, meeting external groups, commuting, traveling, or at home.

Apart from the total, it's the composition of that work time—as well as the time for family, health, and renewal—that is the bigger deal. The way that CEOs choose to allocate their personal presence not only helps determine their effectiveness but also signals to everyone else what is most important. It can have a lot to do with the entire organization's performance.

Given the truth that CEOs are ultimately responsible for the growth of the enterprise, one detail stood out to me.

On average, those CEOs spent just 3 percent of their time with customers. The authors reported that not only were the CEOs surprised by this fact but downright "dismayed."

That is a very limited perspective on the customer's world. The CEOs in the study recognized it, too (which is why they were dismayed). I suspect that every one of those companies has something in their vision or mission statements about customer focus or putting the customer first. Everyone's intentions are good. It is nevertheless true that CEOs, particularly those in larger organizations, are pulled in so many different directions that they have trouble seeing beyond the corporate walls.

The effects can stifle growth plans. Why?

- **You tend to lose the language of the customer over time.** Without much direct contact with customers, it's easy to become mired in the corporate and/or industry lingo that you hear instead.

- **You can focus too much on internal processes, and not enough on consumers' decision-making processes.** If the CEO is getting reports only on the sales funnel and volume of activity (e.g., the number of calls being made), then there is little opportunity to even consider whether those activities match what consumers need to hear and know along their path.

- **You can pay too much attention to anecdotes.** If CEOs have access to only a few snapshots with customers, those interactions will have a disproportionate influence on their view of the market. That's a natural recency effect from the latest meeting that can hang on your brain. But what if those customer interactions aren't a fair representation of reality? In my experience, a customer will behave differently in a conversation involving the CEO than in more normal, everyday cases.

Whether you're managing a large group, a smaller group, or mostly just yourself, recognize that the daily grind is working against your hopes for a vibrant, widely shared message that drives growth. We need to recognize the roadblocks so that you and your organization can get around them—faster and more smoothly than the competition does.

YOU CAN GET EVERYONE AROUND THE ROADBLOCKS

If we consider organizational growth to be a journey, we also should plan for the predictable fact that our road will never be completely smooth.

When it comes to managing your message, the goal is to create and reinforce an environment that fuels growth over the long haul. Therefore, we take as given that there will be sporadic and one-time occurrences to deal with (such as the deer running across your road at dusk or the flash flood during a summer rainstorm) but strategically choose to focus more on the chronic, systemic problems that require proactive navigation. Think of infrastructure bottlenecks that are part of a system (such as the point where a four-lane road becomes a two-lane bridge). This is a scenario that a group of commuters might have to deal with every workday. For a few of them, it will be a regular opportunity to get frustrated. Why not plan an alternative route?

In our case, the roadblocks are a product not of concrete and steel but of psychological and organizational forces. They will be lurking along the road for as long as humans are involved in the business. The most common ones I see (let's call them "The Five Cs") will likely feel familiar to you. Let's call them out and identify some ideas for getting around them nimbly.

The Messaging Roadblock of Consistency

We value consistency in other people, because it signals that we can depend on them. We know what to expect. As customers, we likewise value consistency in organizations. It's comforting to get a consistent message whether we are dealing online, over the phone, or in person. I enjoy hearing Chick-fil-A employees respond to my "thank you" with a "my pleasure" every time.

Contrast that with the scene I witnessed not long ago while boarding a commercial flight. We passengers were going through the usual motions. A man was placing his bag into the overhead bin.

A flight attendant came up and said, "Sir, you can't put your bag there."

The passenger replied, "It's okay. It fits just fine."

The flight attendant said, "No, you can't put it there. It is an FAA regulation and could mean a $25,000 fine."

The passenger was not being combative. He seemed genuinely confused. "The gate agent said just 30 seconds ago that I could bring this aboard."

The flight attendant was getting louder. "I'm telling you that you need to go back up there and check the bag." As the flight attendant walked away, she said to no one in particular (but loud enough for dozens of passengers to hear), "There's always one idiot on every flight."

By the way, this exchange happened in first class. It was much more profound and costly than if a fast-food employee forgot to say the right thing.

The most common frustration I hear from organizational leaders relates to inconsistency in how employees talk about the business and interact with customers. (This is the "Cowboys" symptom of a messaging problem, introduced in Chapter 1.) Leaders recoil at inconsistency because it is the mortal enemy of growth. You need consistency in order to scale.

The consistency roadblock has a number of sources. One is the natural desire of employees and others to exert free will and say things their way. Another is turnover in the organization; when new people enter or are constantly moving into new roles, they lack the knowledge of what to do or how to coach others.

The way to get around the consistency roadblock is to have one central messaging resource. And that resource should not be some overprogrammed, dense set of guidelines that employees will ignore with delight. The type of resource that will actually get used—and thus create more consistency across the organization—will be in a playbook format. Keep it clear, simple, accessible, updated, and tailored to specific roles and conversations. That should winnow the idiotic messages.

The Messaging Roadblock of Comfort

La-Z-Boy sells a lot of recliners. I don't believe they win a lot of design awards, but then again their customers likely put a low priority on being fashion-forward in the family room. The recliner buyer wants to be comfortable, and those big cushy chairs can indeed deliver comfort. My dad needed a darn good reason to get out of his recliner.

As much as we talk about the need for constant change, most of us naturally gravitate to the familiar and comfortable. In business conversations, people tend to talk about what they know best with the people who make them feel comfortable. That means most people in your organization are probably talking about themselves, the company, and the products or services with which they are most familiar. That also means they're likely talking to the same people—at networking events, at industry conferences, at the companies they call on, and away from work. Even worse, most people tend to use the jargon of their field, even if it is incomprehensible or uninteresting to those outside the tribe.

Is it any wonder that, when asked "What's new?" many people reflexively say, "Not much"?

There are several ways to avoid the comfort roadblock. One is to socialize the change that you are making to the organization's message. Let it be known that this is something everyone is doing. Talk about it at regular meetings, during corporate events, and across internal communication channels. Show examples. Take pictures. Another effective tactic is to create and share stories. As you saw in Chapter 4, our brains are wired to pay extra attention to stories and even to share them. That helps, because chances are there actually is something that's new around your business.

The Messaging Roadblock of Complexity

Years ago, people joked that the world had become so complicated we were destined to live with our VCRs blinking "12:00." Now, some might long for the simplicity of that VCR. Am I the only one who relies on his teenagers to troubleshoot technical issues in the home?

Today's products and solutions are so complicated that they put tremendous pressure on both buyers and sellers. No buyer wants to be stuck with something that won't work or that won't integrate with what they already have and understand.

The way to get around the complexity roadblock is to focus on the message itself. Simple language (free of acronyms and jargon) works best. So do pictures. I find that consumers, when presented with complex messages and several options, typically will not ask a clarifying question. They don't want to appear inadequate. That is why many organizations aren't even aware that their messages cause consumers to tune out.

The Messaging Roadblock of Coaching

There is an old management maxim that the easiest way to ruin good workers is to make them managers. This maxim rings true because we see many otherwise capable people struggle with the transition to managing other people. Their performance and motivation decline while their stress levels rise. What happened?

Some workers are promoted because they performed well in functional roles. Others might have been promoted because of tenure in the job or organizational seniority. Sometimes, workers are promoted simply because they are liked (and no other great alternatives were available).

Whatever the source, I see a severe lack of coaching skills and experience in many organizations. In those cases, employees might not feel that anyone is taking a personal interest in their success. Importantly, no one is offering them specific and empathetic guidance in the "how" of their jobs.

In order to avoid this roadblock, organizations need to "coach the coaches." Managers are unsure of what to do because they received little or no training in customer conversations themselves. Many companies are breaking this unfortunate cycle by introducing some form of certification—a process for coaching and evaluation that establishes a minimum level of competency in customer conversations.

Certification requires investment, but it tends to pay off both for new managers and those who have been around a while.

The Messaging Roadblock of Culture

Your organization either supports great messaging or undercuts it. The truth is somewhere in that seemingly mysterious thing known as "our culture."

I believe culture is itself something to be defined and managed. The legendary consultant Alan Weiss (a mentor of mine) offers a pithy definition: culture is *the behavioral manifestation of values.*

To put it another way, I see values as the shared sense of what is important and what is right. Your culture is the set of processes, habits, and interactions that make values play out (or not) in the work environment. For example, if "putting the customer first," "listening to the customer," and "customer centricity" have been publicly declared as organizational values, does the culture reflect that? A healthy culture for supporting customer engagement will emphasize learning, drive the sharing of best practices, encourage innovative approaches, tolerate occasional stumbles on the path toward progress, and celebrate successes.

THE INFLECTION POINTS THAT NEED YOUR ATTENTION

There is never a bad time to get serious about managing your message. As you have seen, every organization has multiple opportunities every day to be a part of growth conversations.

Human nature being what it is, however, most of us need the occasional kick in the rear to make a big change (look—it's that pesky "Comfort" roadblock again!). Something makes us look at the status quo in a new way. Some external force prompts a greater sense of urgency.

What is most likely to get you off cruise control? For some leaders, it might be the disappointment of poor performance. For others, it might be something new in the organization (such as an acquisition, new products, or new distribution capabilities). Sometimes there is big news to share. For example, in the US beverage industry, carbonated soft drinks have been the leader for decades. Their market share has been declining, however, as bottled water has been ascending. During 2017, the sales lines crossed—making bottled water the number one beverage category in the country. As you might imagine, the leadership of the International Bottled Water Association (IBWA) got pretty excited. The chairwoman, Shayron Barnes-Selby, wanted to make sure that all member companies were sharing this news with their customers. In the ensuing September/October 2017 issue of the IBWA's magazine *Bottled Water Reporter,* she exhorted members to "shout it from the rooftops and share the good news" (p. 2). When I was invited to speak at the IBWA's annual conference, I reminded the members that they should not stop with a message from the rooftops; because so many of them are involved in home and office delivery, they can share the news *under* millions of rooftops as well. But they would need to equip their route drivers, call center employees, and account managers to do so.

Let's take note of some common inflection points that, for you and/or your business, should prompt a fresh look at your message:

For You

- Just getting started professionally (e.g., graduating)

- Returning to the workforce after a substantial period of time

- Making a big change (e.g., starting a new role, entering a different industry, upgrading your professional identity)

FOR YOUR ORGANIZATION

- A startup that needs to establish awareness and identity

- A rebranding effort

- Experiencing fast growth, bringing in new people

- Announcing a new leadership team

- Dealing with high turnover in key positions

- Adding to the portfolio of products or solutions available

- Serving new or additional markets (e.g., new type of customer, expanded locations)

- Introducing new ways of serving customers (e.g., online offerings, new distribution or sales partners)

HOW TO GET CHANGE RIGHT

There is a proverbial elephant in the room when leaders are considering major change initiatives. They know how difficult change can be and that it typically doesn't work as hoped.

In an arresting *Harvard Business Review* article back in 2000 ("Cracking the Code of Change"), Nitin Nohria and Michael Beer reported that 70 percent of corporate change initiatives fail. I have seen no research recently that would suggest things are much different today.

How can you improve your odds? One way is to consider the input from those who would bear the burden of implementing said changes. I can offer some insights from frontline employees in a company that was both changing its solutions (one of the major categories listed earlier) and the message strategy around them.

Here was the situation. This particular company is large and dispersed, selling high-tech products and services to other businesses. Their marketing change was twofold: move from selling a wide range of offerings to a smaller set of more integrated solutions, and learn how to engage potential buyers at a higher, more executive level. We had established a core working group of employees, from across business units, who together were helping to craft both the offerings and the new messages.

As we prepared to get the new stuff ready for teams across the globe, we asked the group this open-ended question: "What do you see as the keys to making changes stick over the long term?" We told the group that we would report their opinions, without individual attribution, back to executive leadership.

Their responses fell into four categories:

- **Management focus and reinforcement.** The team recommended well-defined performance goals (including compensation and incentives that would reward change behavior), help for middle managers as they prepare to coach their direct reports, and recognition by management of early adopters.

- **A clear roadmap for success.** Team members said they wanted a playbook that would be easily accessible, a clear solution/product roadmap so that everyone would know what would be available, and when; training specific to the change initiative; and assurance that technical resources would be available as needed.

- **A customer-engagement strategy aligned across units.** We heard that management should minimize silos, place emphasis on higher-level customer and growth goals, help account managers understand how to prioritize opportunities, and involve other parts of the business, including distributors and delivery partners.

- **Support for the long haul.** Team members said that managers should keep proof points, case studies, and stories current; include the change initiative in onboarding activities for new employees; provide regular reporting of results compared to goals; share progress regularly; and provide clearly defined accountabilities for "who does what."

It's my experience that, if you make sure change is planned with the changees in mind, then your probability of success will rise above the 30 percent average.

THE AMAZING (AND FREE!) AMPLIFIER OF ACKNOWLEDGMENT

Interested in a simple way to personally provide effective message leadership—one that is proven to work but won't cost you a dime? You can thank me later.

There is now mounting evidence that gratitude on the job has very tangible benefits for those expressing thanks as well as those receiving it.

According to a survey of 2,000 adults (reported in the *Greater Good* magazine from the Greater Good Science Center at the University of California-Berkeley), Americans are pretty good about expressing thanks and doing so for altruistic reasons. About six in ten adults say they show gratitude daily to their spouse, whereas nearly half express gratitude daily to other members of their immediate families. The vast majority (92 percent) say they have been feeling the same or higher levels of gratitude over the last few years.

Do most people express gratitude in the hopes of getting something in return? When asked in the survey why they gave thanks, people were more than twice as likely to choose options related to the greater good (e.g., "it makes the world a better place") than to choose options related to reciprocity (e.g., "other people will be nicer to me").

That's encouraging news. Still, the workplace is a venue where expressions of gratitude are far less likely to happen. Only one in seven Americans gives thanks on a daily basis to friends or work colleagues. More than one-third of those surveyed said they never have thanked a boss.

Clearly, there is room for a "gratitude adjustment" on the job. If you can lead such a change in behavior within your business, be prepared for an uptick in effort and productivity as well.

I recently saw an example of the power of gratitude in marketing and sales, in the form of field research led by Francesca Gino of Harvard Business School. Dr. Gino tested these effects with forty-one fundraisers at a university (all of whom were working on fixed salaries). For half of the group, the development director visited them in person to say, "I am very grateful for your hard work. We sincerely appreciate your contributions to the university." The other half of the group received no extra expression of thanks. During the next week, the experimental group (who received direct thanks) increased the number of calls they made by 50 percent, whereas the control group made the same number of calls as they had the previous week.

If you have a sales or development operation, wouldn't you be interested in driving 50 percent higher activity levels just from the power of your words?

There are substantial benefits to the thanks-giver as well. According to a research program from Sonja Lyubomirsky, people motivated to express thanks on a regular basis also feel more optimistic, are more satisfied with their lives, show fewer physical symptoms (such as headaches, acne, or nausea), and even exercise more often.

What is the best way to start? In a series of studies, Lyubomirsky had participants literally count their blessings. She directed people to keep a journal, writing down and thinking about five things for which they were grateful. Those who were intentional about counting their blessings (compared to a control group directed to simply "think about five daily hassles or five life events that had happened to them") experienced those wonderful health and psychological benefits.

To fine-tune the analysis, Lyubomirsky and her team next wanted to learn how often the blessing count should occur. One group of participants updated their gratitude journals on a weekly basis (Sunday nights only), and a second group made entries three times per week (Tuesday, Thursday, and Sunday). Interestingly enough, those who counted their blessings once per week gained far greater benefits—likely because doing so more frequently became a ritual or chore rather than an opportunity for deeper reflection.

YOUR MESSENGERS WILL APPRECIATE THE GUIDANCE

Back in my own professor days, students would ask me a lot of questions. The three most common were "Will this be on the test?", "Do I have to come to all of the classes?", and "Will you be a reference for me?" The first two were, I must admit, annoying and at times discouraging. The third was different. It was a legitimate request for help from someone who was motivated to succeed.

When asked to produce a message for someone else's benefit, I wanted to do it right. I would ask the student a few questions about his or her goals, the audience, and any particular characteristics or talking points to include. Often I would ask the student to draft a letter that I could edit and sign.

Come to think of it, when I asked my own professors for similar help long ago, they did the same things!

We see similar patterns today within online platforms such as LinkedIn. Things there are in ready-to-serve formats—either on the light side (endorsements of someone's specific skills or competencies, where all one needs to do is check a box) or in a more tailored way (recommendations that may be written in draft form for the benefit of the would-be recommender). LinkedIn makes it easy to say nice things about someone else, jumping past the uncomfortable "what would you like me to say" part.

The people you ask to talk on behalf of your business will, very likely, be happy to help. At the same time, they will appreciate some guidance. A blank slate is stressful and time-consuming.

The unfortunate fact is that millions of smart and accomplished people struggle to talk about their own work, much less someone else's. How bad is it out there? I once saw, in an online discussion group for marketing research professionals, where the group moderator posed this question: "How do you introduce yourself at a cocktail party?" Many dozens of these professionals responded in a public forum for their peers to see.

Understand that these professionals know their stuff. In order to do their jobs well, they need to be good with research design, analysis, and interpretation. Many of them are freelancers or are part of small firms, so they need to be able to talk about their work in order to land projects. That's why their collective responses to the "how you introduce yourself" question were so enlightening.

Here are three of the responses, with names omitted (you will understand why):

- I introduce myself by saying, "In a nutshell, we provide market intelligence that supports key business decisions, providing the company with data-driven analysis and recommendations to know in our market, identify gaps, and maximize revenues."

- I tell them, "You know those annoying people who call you at dinner time and want to ask you 100 questions about your cereal? Yep, that's me."

- If anyone asks, I'm a butcher.

Ouch. Here we have professionals proudly sharing how they sound like a brochure, introduce themselves as an annoying person, or hide from their profession altogether. Can you see how lots of people need a messaging leader who will encourage them and model good practice?

GETTING READY TO RUN

In your organization, you might be surrounded by valuable people with good intentions who similarly lack confidence and skill in talking about themselves and the business. They will appreciate some guidance or structure—not a script, but something that takes the anxiety and guesswork out of everyday business conversations.

Similarly, there are likely many people outside of the organization who are willing to serve as messengers. Social psychologist Heidi Grant has a program of research that reminds us of several truths (which might have become lost in our selfie age). Most people buy into the idea of helpfulness, and they don't like to say no when there is a request for help. We tend to underestimate by roughly half how likely it is that other people will help us. You just need to make your request clear, specific, and easy. In most cases, not only will people follow through on such a request, but you will also make the relationship a little stronger in the process.

You can play an important leadership role even if you aren't the messaging expert yourself. As you will see in the next chapter, it just takes some structure, a good example, and supportive coaching.

I once had the good intention to run a marathon. I had never done anything like that before, but it seemed like a laudable goal. Then the reality of the time and training required began to sink in. Oh, and I wanted to survive the process.

Fortunately, I found a great group of experienced runners who agreed to let a newbie train with them. Their mantra was "plan your run, and run your plan." The plan was a detailed schedule for training. There was an important social and bonding component, too. The group would join together for "long runs" early on weekend mornings, and occasionally get together to share stories and encourage one another.

There were low points, to be sure. Once I remember treating my aches and pains after making it through a nine mile-long run, the longest distance I had ever gone. I realized that run represented only about one-third the distance of a marathon.

Eventually I did complete the New York Marathon with the group—and about 28,000 other runners—and even made my time goal. Obviously, I survived (although my back, knees, and feet discouraged the rest of me from ever running a marathon again).

Let's cover how to plan your run and run your plan—not as a one-time effort but in a sustainable way. Everyone can make it to the finish line.

TAKE A MANAGER MOMENT . . .

- Consider the managers in your organization. Do they generally have training in customer-level conversation? Are there any skill gaps to address with them?

- If your organization is in a state of change, what are employees saying about it? Do they understand the reasons for change? Is the leadership committed to providing the messaging tools, support, and encouragement to help make these needed changes stick?

- How are the organization's managers expressing their appreciation today? Are they being specific and public?

9

KNOW, GO, AND SHOW:
How Great Leaders Become
Great Coaches, Too

THIS CHAPTER IS ABOUT THE qualities in leadership and coaching that provide positive, lasting change. The title comes from something author and speaker John C. Maxwell said: "A leader is one who knows the way, goes the way, and shows the way." Even that succinct definition includes the connection of leadership to coaching.

To this point we have generally focused on the things that people need to know about their message and messengers, including the most powerful words to use, ways to turn complex and technical information into engaging stories, and the inherent strengths most people naturally have for conversation. Yet message leadership is about more than knowing the right information or identifying efficient processes. It must also include some "go" (modeling the right behaviors for others) and some "show" (equipping others with the tools and confidence to do it themselves).

The CEO of a Fortune 500 company had a reputation among employees for his communication skills, including a provocative elevator pitch. I asked one of the senior vice presidents how much of the CEO's message she used herself. "None at all," she said. "That's his pitch. He talks to different people than I do. And I could never do it the way he does."

This CEO was a great messenger, but he wanted his executive team to step up as well. We had to work on ways of taking the best of what he did, translating and tailoring it for different executives, and getting them comfortable.

At least that CEO was visible and consistent with his message. Every time he did so, he sent a strong signal that conversational fluency was vital to executives' performance. He also spoke all around the company and its many locations—demonstrating through his deeds that it was important to have your story at the ready, regardless of your tenure or status at the company.

"DO AS I SAY, NOT AS I DO" DIDN'T WORK FOR OUR PARENTS, EITHER

I often smile when I think of how my parents—indeed, how much of their generation—went about their parenting roles. Both of my parents smoked; they got hooked while teenagers and could not kick the habit until late in life. Our family vehicles tended to be the big sedans or wagons (with bench seats covered by vinyl). My mom readily admitted that, if my brother or I were in the front seat, her right arm was the predominant seat belt. There was no liquor cabinet, just an easily accessible shelf in the pantry (although I would never have dared to try sneaking a sip ... my dad would surely have noticed). As teenagers are prone to do, on occasion I might have asked my parents something like, "Why is it that you tell me not to smoke, when you do it yourself?" The answer, said with a straight face, was "Do as I say, not as I do."

My parents did well by my brother and me (probably better than we deserved). Still, there is an important point. In most settings, subordinates pay at least as much attention to what an authority figure does as they do to what he or she says.

If you're in an influential role, make sure your visible behaviors are consistent with stated priorities. Many of the professionals I've met who made good message leaders considered themselves pretty average at communication. Still, they understood that everyone in the organization would look to them for cues as to whether this new initiative on consistent messaging was really a priority. They got out of the office, got away from too many emails and memos, and engaged with people directly. As one said, "It was important to have real conversations about our most important conversations."

PUT ON THE UNIFORM

Dad was a military man. It began for him when he was just a kid, going out of state to a military boarding school. Following college and active duty, he went into the National Guard. He loved it. He even seemed a little different when he wore his uniform. Perhaps it was his cue for good posture and bearing. I remember how impressed my friends were when my dad—a major at the time—donned the uniform for "career day" at my school.

In later years, well after he had retired from the National Guard, I was standing near Dad when he was about to be introduced at a reception. When the person called him "General Karrh," I swear that he stood up two inches taller, reversing years of posture decline.

There is no uniform for a message leader, of course, but it might help some people to imagine that they have one.

There are times when we need to symbolically put on the message leader's uniform. It's for the benefit of others, not just to make you look or feel better.

If you are part of a larger organization, there is an internal audience you need to engage that holds the key to change.

MEET THEM IN THE MIDDLE

Does middle management matter anymore?

That question was posed to me during a podcast. The subject of middle management and its future has been in debate for many years now. As industry after industry has felt the effects of consolidation and disintermediation, the ranks of middle managers have, in many cases, dwindled. Even the culture and language around middle management have changed. "Middle manager" is not generally viewed as a desirable role to have on the way up, but rather as someone who is stuck in a bureaucracy, with some accountability but little control, and facing an uncertain future. Yet, there's plenty of reason to believe that middle management itself is not going away completely any time soon (nor should it).

I see lots of organizations that need effective middle management. They might have operations that are geographically dispersed, are subject to high turnover rates, or require consistently great "high-touch" customer service in order to stay competitive. That's difficult to pull off without a cohort of managers to get new colleagues up to speed, contain tribal knowledge, and keep processes running efficiently. Middle management is also the ranks from which future leadership still tends to come.

If your company is under pressure to change, evolve, and grow, then middle management is likely the key to success. Dr. Behnam Tabrizi of Stanford studied large-scale change and innovation efforts in fifty-six companies across nine industries. The bad news is that most of the change efforts failed. But there was some good news for middle management. In the 32 percent of change efforts that succeeded, a primary success factor was "the involvement of mid-level managers two or more levels below the CEO."

What is the key for getting the most from middle management? Can they be the champions of a new growth message? As companies tend to be leaner and need to be more dynamic, I find that the role of manager needs an amendment. Managers need to learn how to become effective coaches to their direct reports.

I worked with the marketing and sales teams of a company that sells a medical device and services across the United States. Like other industries built on research and technology, this one is changing all the time. As the company's marketing and sales strategies evolved, the leadership team began to see the need for a coaching framework tailored to the needs of its sales managers. Those teams were hearing plenty from the top about the company's vision and "why" of its strategy. What they needed to know was the day-to-day "how." Middle managers are the indispensable link.

In this particular case, the "how" included best practices for prioritizing accounts, initiating conversations, following up, and troubleshooting. Just as with a coach in sports, the role of a manager/coach in business is to extend the culture, build skills, help everyone prepare, and provide specific guidance.

IS YOUR HELP JUST-IN-TIME OR JUST-IN-CASE?

We can't blame managers for feeling frustrated at times. Some spend a lot of time on check-ins and reminders. They wonder why their team members appear to ignore advice and gloss over information presented to them. The right conversations are not happening, and business results suffer. As one exasperated manager put it, "Why don't they get it?"

That is a big question, of course, one that cries out for discovery. But in general, if your team is not accessing the right information or doing what you believe to be the right things, there are some likely suspects:

- They never knew the information in the first place.

- They didn't understand that the activity was actually part of their job or role.

- They didn't feel comfortable.

- They thought that someone else was likely or better suited to handle it.

- *Or just maybe* . . . they had the right intentions but did not have the right information or guidance at the point they needed it.

Messaging opportunities come our way all the time. Some are predictable and even scheduled; you know when they are going to occur and what the setting will be (e.g., a speech, a customer meeting, or a presentation to a community group). But most are less predictable. They might present themselves during work hours or outside of them. They might happen in a hallway or next to a soccer field. That puts more emphasis on planning and consistent practice.

Many organizations have, over time, built large repositories of information. These can feel like smaller-scale Libraries of Congress, containing product information, operating manuals, coaching and scoring systems, case studies, brand guidelines, sales collateral, and on and on. They fit a "just-in-case" model, meaning that there is one central location where you can find everything you might need—just in case you ever need it.

Increasingly, just-in-case messaging information fails to match the way people work and what they need. Everyone is trying to be more agile in their work; they need a slimmed-down, flexible, "just-in-time" alternative.

I recommend a playbook approach because it drives consistency and agility at the same time. Playbooks—the good ones—are built for specific conversations. Users don't waste time combing through less relevant information, and managers can coach to (meaning they can "show") particular competencies. As is the case with the types of playbooks that sports teams use, managers and their teams can practice together efficiently.

Playbooks also seem to fit the coaching patterns of the most effective managers. A 2018 Gartner report identified four categories of managers, according to their coaching styles:

- Teacher managers tend to coach their direct reports according to their own knowledge and experience.

- Always-on managers provide continual coaching (comparable to so-called "helicopter parents").

- Cheerleader managers take a more hands-off approach, allowing employees to direct their own development.

- Connector managers give targeted feedback in their area of expertise, but otherwise connect employees to other members of the team or organization who are better suited to the task.

Cheerleaders are the most common type of manager but not the most effective. That honor goes to the connectors, whose employees are three times more likely to be high performers as are subordinates of the other three types.

A good playbook works particularly well for connectors, because it clarifies and consolidates other sources of messaging information—freeing the connectors to monitor progress without having to teach everything themselves.

THIS ISN'T HIGH SCHOOL: HOW ADULTS LEARN

As organizations strive for an environment of continuous learning, they look for ways to best engage today's worker. One guideline is clear: we need to get learners out of a strict classroom environment.

Those of us who are in business—and have also taught in multiple environments—know the difference. My favorite teaching experiences were probably those in an MBA program where the students were also working full time. They came to class, one night per week, typically straight from their jobs. It could be grueling at times, but these professionals were consistently taking the ideas we discussed about marketing management and applying them on the job each week. The immediate applicability of new knowledge was key. Again, it was "just in time" over "just in case."

Immediate applicability is one characteristic of professional learners. Another is their mindset; adults on the job are not generally learning for the sake of learning. Malcolm Knowles, an adult education expert, developed theories of "andragogy" (which he defined as "the art and science of helping adults learn"). The result was six principles of adults when it comes to their learning:

- They are internally motivated and self-directed.

- They bring their life experience into learning experiences

- They are goal oriented.

- They look for relevance.

- They are practical.

- They like to be respected.

When it comes to playbook content and coaching practices, keep it practical and allow employees to bring some of their interpretation and experiences into the mix.

DO THEY REALLY WANT YOUR FEEDBACK? YES, THEY DO

In order for messaging coaching to work consistently, several things need to happen. There should be a sound framework for coaching activities, for example. Managers and employees need that playbook so that everyone has clear, concise, updated information at the right times. Managers should adopt a "connector" mindset to every degree possible. Oh, lest we forget, the employees must be coachable! Many managers wonder whether that is true, especially where younger workers have become the majority group in the organization. They might assume that Millennials want autonomy and do-it-yourself options, as opposed to coaching sessions with their supervisors.

Well, there is good news. Millennial workers are not only open to more coaching and feedback, they are asking for it. A global survey of 1,400 Millennials revealed some surprises concerning their desire for coaching:

- Millennials want more feedback than what they are getting now. On average, Millennials want feedback at least monthly. Unfortunately, only 46 percent agreed that their managers were meeting their expectations for feedback.

- Millennials want feedback 50 percent more frequently than do their more senior counterparts.

- The environment for coaching Millennials might need some adjustments. Although Millennials are asking for more feedback, they aren't looking for controlled messages or scheduled performance reviews. They prefer private coaching in real time. And they value authenticity from their supervisors.

Got it, Coach?

NOW YOU'RE READY!

Let's summarize a few of the considerations you have seen when it comes to your new growth message and how to spread it. First, there are many reasons that organizations might feel compelled to get more strategic about their everyday messaging. Typically, something important is changing in the business and/or its operating environment. The messaging needs to work for the strategy going forward.

The traditional way of approaching new messaging has been to treat it as a sort of short-term campaign. That typically leads to disappointment. A lot of time and money might be poured into message development, collateral, events, training, and a motivational kickoff, but the story fizzles out after a few months. There's no competitive advantage to be had.

A more strategic approach—one that increases the likelihood of achieving growth targets—is not a promotional campaign but rather a new competency, spread across the organization, designed to stick for the long term.

Here is an example of leadership and coaching that hit its intended mark. A client company needed help with communicating a series of product launches. Many of the new products represented substantially different types of solutions or pricing models for the teams. Responding to changes in competition and in customers' needs, the company's management team was determined to not only bump up revenue but also to drive some long-term, internal changes at the same time.

This client follows a change management model popularized by Harvard Business School professor John Kotter. The logic and sequence of the model matches those situations I've seen over the years when leadership was able to drive some positive change that lasted for years.

Kotter's model follows this eight-stage sequence:

- **Create urgency.** According to Kotter, the first step is also the most difficult. Most of us resist change. To overcome that inertia, the teams need to both get the change imperative intellectually and feel the urgency in their guts. Kotter suggests that at least three-quarters of the leadership must truly buy into the need for change. Which leads to . . .

- **Form a powerful coalition.** You'll need a team. Change champions might not always be in the most obvious or highest places on the organizational chart. In our team's consulting engagements, we typically select a team of high performers (with "street cred") from different units and with different tenures in the company.

- **Create a vision for change.** Everyone needs to know more than just "the status quo isn't working anymore." (By itself, that tends to induce anxiety.) They need a simple, achievable, and compelling view of your destination, something the leadership team and change champions can be comfortable in sharing in two minutes or less (a PowerPoint deck is decidedly not the answer here).

- **Communicate the vision.** Your champions should be sharing the vision at every opportunity—not just at kickoffs or regular meetings. The group will need to compare notes along the way.

- **Remove obstacles.** The barriers to change may be human, structural, informational, and/or embedded within incentive systems. For human obstacles, the leader's role is twofold: get key current employees on board, and bring in change instigators as needed.

- **Create short-term wins.** People will look for evidence that the change initiative is going to succeed or fail. You'll need one or more early wins that are fairly easy and inexpensive, and that don't depend on the involvement of internal critics.

- **Build on the change.** Some will declare victory prematurely. The natural temptation is to take a long, deep breath and move from discomfort to comfort again. Savvy executives will over time bring in fresh change agents who don't own the initiatives that worked well yesterday (while still celebrating the contributions of that original team).

- **Anchor the change in your organization's culture.** This includes sharing success stories as well as embedding lessons learned into onboarding and training activities.

Not long ago, I spoke with a senior manager at another company that had introduced new messaging internally. At first there had been some heartburn; the leadership wondered whether they could avoid the comfort roadblock, especially with employees who had been around for years. "You know, Jim, it just gets easier as we go," he said. This was good news. I attribute it to good leadership.

The new message itself wasn't pushed from the top or farmed out to an agency. It was instead developed by people from across the company.

When it was time for training, people weren't herded into a classroom. They went through the experience as intact teams, learning together and planning to apply the message as soon as they returned to work.

Managers coached. They led practice sessions in teams and individually so that people could build their skills and confidence.

Managers shared insights and successes so that no one felt as if they were going it alone.

When you begin to manage your message, you might have a little heartburn as well. But know that it will get easier and feel more normal. After a while, you won't even have to act as the message leader all of the time; your messengers will begin to manage themselves.

In the final chapter, you can see how several professionals and organizations, in varying degrees of change, have all managed to make theirs work.

10

BUILD MOMENTUM AND
ENJOY THE BUSINESS IMPACT

THERE ARE MANY WAYS that managing your message can help your business—and even you personally.

Over the years I have seen different ways that organizations have tracked their improvement:

- Sales and growth metrics such as volume, margins, win rates, and time needed to close deals

- Customer-level metrics of loyalty, referrals, or satisfaction

- Operational and HR metrics like time to productivity and employee engagement

- Communication metrics such as brand strength or corporate reputation

Plus, there are benefits more difficult to quantify yet no less real for today's professional—benefits such as less stress, more recognition, and greater clarity.

Because every person and organization is in a different place—with varying starting points, strengths, resources, and growth strategies—there isn't a common scorecard.

Nor is there one overriding impetus that might spur you to action (as was the case with the "Y2K" scare, for those who might remember . . . the rest of you can Google it).

You might be feeling the stress of crickets chirping and thus the imperative to grow and equip your clan of messengers. Perhaps you are tired of the inconsistency in how people talk about your business, how the language on your website is different than in everyday conversation, and on and on. Maybe you have a gnawing sense that your message fails to stand out—that you are more like a part of the noise than a clear signal to your customers and prospects.

Most of us respond better to stories than to scorecards. I offer these stories of real people who, to some degree, have used the power of their message to drive change and growth. How have I come to know these stories? Some are clients. Some are friends. In one case, I was told about the person but never met him. There is even a story about me, years ago—messing up royally but then getting some timeless advice worth sharing. I selected these stories to represent a range of professions, organizations, and scenarios. You'll likely feel a connection to at least one of them.

KEEP GROWING THROUGH GENERATIONAL CHANGE

Most family businesses struggle when the founder is no longer in the picture. Researchers consistently report that only about one-third of family-owned businesses survive the transition from the first to the second generation (which means that two-thirds do not). I find a similar challenge in companies begun by dynamic, charismatic leaders with big visions; in their absence, there is often a giant vacuum that cannot be filled. ATA International (formerly the American

Taekwondo Association) had both of those going on at the same time.

Haeng Ung (H. U.) Lee was born in China and relocated with his family to Korea before he was a teenager. He began training in the martial arts, joined the Korean Army as a trainer, and later opened a taekwondo school at Osan Air Force Base. Lee trained and befriended an American serviceman, Richard Reed, who later helped Lee relocate to America. Lee and Reed opened a martial arts school in Omaha, Nebraska. Lee had an enormous vision for a network of schools across the United States. He founded the American Taekwondo Association in 1969, became an American citizen in 1973, and soon began developing a new Songham philosophy of taekwondo that would be taught in his rapidly growing network.

Lee's vision was global, and he maintained strong ties to Korea. He moved the ATA's international headquarters to Little Rock, Arkansas, in large part because the landscape reminded him of his Korean homeland.

How strong was the bond between Lee and the ATA community? In 1990, Lee tested for the distinguished rank of Ninth Degree Black Belt; a petition signed by more than 100,000 ATA members honored him with the title of Grand Master.

When H. U. Lee passed away in 2000, he was given the posthumous title of Eternal Grand Master. But what about the business of the ATA? By that time, two partner organizations had been established that grew schools and memberships around the world. The schools were not franchises controlled from headquarters but independently owned and operated licensed facilities.

A decade after the death of Eternal Grand Master Lee, ATA International was at an important crossroads. (Full disclosure: At this point I was engaged by the ATA leadership as an adviser.) Lee's brothers were highly accomplished taekwondo masters in their own right. The key role of Grand Master was in transition from one of the surviving brothers to another. The challenge was keeping the original vision together despite generational change, disparate parts of the organization, and dramatic changes among consumers (i.e., what families were demanding).

When you expect different groups of messengers to eventually be on the same page—especially if there is separation by location, business unit, tenure, even language—it's important to involve people from those different groups in the creating the message itself. Even when people believe in the overall vision, they will have different interpretations and sometimes competing opinions on how to find success. They need to see their fingerprints (or at least the fingerprints of people like them) on the process. That leads to a greater likelihood of acceptance or buy-in.

In the case of the ATA, there was an existing organizational and cultural structure—the Masters Council—that could operate at the heart of the process. Members of the Masters Council had earned very high rank and respect within Songham taekwondo. They also tended to be school owners, so they were close to their customers and communities. The council drove decisions on testing and training (including communications) for the new Grand Master as well as external messaging to the ATA community worldwide.

That process happened nearly a decade ago as of this writing. ATA International is now transitioning to its fourth Grand Master, following the precedent set before. As it nears its fiftieth anniversary, it reports more than 130,000 active members training and competing around the world.

ATA International continues to beat the odds (in this case, even with bare hands and feet) by keeping its community involved in the message.

ACCELERATING THE GROWTH OF YOUR GREAT IDEA

You might have a great business model, one that has even had some early success. Both your brain and your gut are sure that your business is different and better than what customers have been able to buy in the past. To you it doesn't seem risky but rather highly logical. And while we recognize the value of patience, it can nevertheless be frustrating when the market doesn't appear to "get" the idea as quickly as you know is possible.

This was part of the picture with Arkansas Mutual Insurance Company (AMIC), the new kid on the block in its state. Most insurance companies have been around since dinosaurs roamed the Earth, or so it seems; AMIC, on the other hand, was founded in 2007. For its first few years, it was too small for the major rating organization A. M. Best to even consider giving an A rating. It also was a niche player, member-owned and focused solely on medical malpractice insurance for doctors in one state.

For most of us, insurance companies are not the prototypical topic of conversation (unless something is wrong). Despite the other headwinds they faced, AMIC's leadership had some unusual opportunities. As you saw in Chapter 2, three words (*you, more, new*) have proven popular and effective in marketing for decades. The company certainly stood out in terms of *new*. AMIC also had a core message about *you*; malpractice insurance is a very big deal to physicians, and not just financially. It strikes a personal chord to the very identity and reputation of the profession. The mutual model excludes outside shareholders.

I was engaged to help with messaging and soon was invited to a board meeting. The board members—physicians, business leaders, and industry experts—were dressed casually that Saturday morning because most would be attending a big college football game in the afternoon. As you might imagine, there would be rampant tailgating and lots of catching up with peers and friends. Many of those people were likely to be physicians, practice managers, hospital administrators, and other influencers.

I posed a question: "When you're asked about what is new, or what you have been up to since the last time you and the other person were together, what will you say about this company?" There was a period of silence around the table. Everyone knew so much about the business, and cared so much about it, that there would almost be too many things to say! But that moment also helped to reinforce the need for consistency within the core group—and the benefits of being ready to say the right things at the right times.

The company was courted by several potential partners. Eventually they voted to become a subsidiary of Constellation, a large mutual holding company. With its added scale, AMIC received its A. M. Best rating—and a jump in interest from insurance agencies who wanted to sell the company's policies.

If what you sell is seen to varying degrees as risky, expensive, and/or personally important, then your messengers have an irreplaceable role in growth. The consistency of their message will go a long way in helping you seem less risky. Active listening will help, too. Welcome the objections. Over time, your conversations will help you stand out from the entrenched dinosaurs.

GETTING EVERYONE UP TO SPEED FASTER

Opower was a young company in a hurry. They were "running the largest behavioral science experiment in the world" and needed more of their people to be able to explain this to potential customers.

Co-founder Alex Laskey explained the idea in a TEDx talk and other public forums. Opower created software and sold its use to utility companies that, in turn, had aggressive goals for helping reduce energy consumption. Through the utilities' monthly bills sent to its customers, Opower delivered personalized home energy reports. Those reports were different—not just comparing energy use to the previous month or year, but also showing people how their consumption compared to their neighbors'. There were also specific recommendations to help save energy in their homes.

That was heady stuff. But Opower's sales effort was under strain. Their customers were not the end users but rather utilities trying to hit energy-efficiency targets. The company was bringing in new people—mostly young and from outside the utilities industry—so their challenges involved both the message itself as well as consistency. Which insights and stories would help these relative newbies connect with managers at utilities? How could they get everyone behind the message, quickly? (Full disclosure time: Opower was a client of DSG, where I serve as a consulting principal. I created a sales messaging playbook in concert with the DSG and Opower teams.)

Opower had a larger initiative to scale their sales organization and take advantage of market demand. Their ideas could seem complicated. They were the disruptors in a utilities industry driven by more traditional thinking.

One technique that helped was whiteboarding. As you saw in Chapter 4, a simple visual can lower the "fear factor" inherent in bold new ideas. With the Opower leadership, we created a visual conversation (among other messaging tools) that helped sales reps get away from technical descriptions and software demonstrations. That in turn helped Opower's message get past their audiences' Lizard Brains.

With this clearer story and a messaging playbook available, it took about 25 percent less time for sales reps to be productive. Managers had less worry about sending new sales reps into executive-level meetings. Everything accelerated. Opower held an IPO (initial public offering) in 2014 and was acquired by Oracle two years later.

If your business idea is new and potentially confusing, make sure you are creating the right conversational environment. Prospective customers will have questions, objections, and anxieties. A one-way presentation or demonstration does not allow enough space for you to help bring those into the open. You might have the coolest and most technically sound solution in the history of such things, but unless the prospective customer believes it will work in her world she will remain a prospect.

It also pays to simplify. That makes it easier for messengers of all stripes to share your great idea faster.

MAKING A RADICAL CHANGE IN PROFESSIONAL IDENTITY

By her own admission, she "didn't like birds." Yet somehow Andie Cohen-Healy wound up starting a business combining fashion and bird feathers.

After many years in New York City, Andie moved to California in order to be with her soon-to-be husband. When the two of them were moving into their new house, they were surprised to find two chicks were included as a gift from the previous owners. Nothing in Andie's background (she grew up in New Jersey) had prepared her to be a chicken owner. Yet by the fourth day Andie "had fallen in chicken love."

Andie had quickly come around to liking birds, but she didn't like her job. It was a toxic situation. Andie's creative talents—including experience with the Leo Burnett advertising agency in Chicago and managing satellite operations for MTV in New York—weren't being used. Then along came serendipity.

As a later-in-life bride, Andie did not want the typical items (what she called "bridal blah") for her wedding day. Instead, she wanted some special touch that reflected her personality and self-assurance. By that time Andie and her groom had five spoiled pet chickens; she first thought about carrying a bouquet of their feathers down the aisle. But then came the "Eureka!" moment. Why not create a bridal headpiece using those colorful plumes? She crafted a chicken/ostrich feather, organza, and pearl fascinator that gained so many compliments Andie became convinced there was a market for one-of-a-kind hair ornaments for brides and party-goers. She launched The Feathered Head, with its mission to make women look and feel singularly beautiful.

Andie was in a new place, and with a new business—one with no connection to her recent experience. How could she find her audience, or rather allow her audience to find her? Certainly her product and message were "new" and distinctive (we saw the importance of this in Chapter 2). As it turned out, Andie had the elements to be an effective messenger. "I found that I was using those things I had learned along the way . . . how to get noticed, how to pitch," she told me. She hired a freelance publicist to gain access to the media outlets where brides and party-goers gathered—but made the pitches herself.

Now the business has been named a "Top 10 Favorite" by the LA Fashion District and has been featured in the *Los Angeles Times* Style section; one of Andie's hats even made *The Today Show* during a Royal Wedding. Andie understands her customers' desire for style and individuality and has maintained that well-focused message. If you do likewise, regardless of background, you can earn a feather in your cap. (Sorry.)

Many professionals make transitions that are more evolutionary than revolutionary; they take the expertise from a familiar domain into a new one. For example, people regularly transition from the military to civilian life or from the for-profit world to a nonprofit. In such a case, it's vital to not only identify the skills and benefits that transfer from your former world but also find a message that resonates with audiences in your new one. That can be a challenge when you have been steeped in a certain lingo for years.

Chip Massey had spent more than two decades as an FBI Special Agent and hostage/crisis negotiator. In that role, he collaborated with the CIA to crack espionage rings, conducted counter-terrorism investigations, and worked in intense situations such as international kidnappings and fugitive apprehensions. That's the stuff of movies and TV shows. Chip's time in the FBI was itself the product of a career shift; he had served for several years as a Methodist minister. His personal story is inherently interesting. Yet, as Chip planned to make the transition to a business consultant, there was a messaging challenge: he would need to "connect the dots" for his potential clients and verbalize how the skills he used in his previous, mysterious worlds could directly apply to their everyday worlds.

The audience for Chip's conversations would include corporate executives and sales managers. Chip decided to frame the benefits of working with him in language such as "becoming an active listener," "instantly building rapport," and "succeeding in high-stakes negotiations." These are not only desirable and understandable outcomes for his prospective clients, but also clearly linked to his rather unique competencies. Even after the initial "wow" factor of learning from a real-life hostage negotiator has subsided, Chip maintains a message in the customer's language.

WHEN YOU'RE JUST GETTING STARTED

Can you create a great personal message if you have limited or even zero direct experience? When you are going into the professional world for the first time—or perhaps for the first time in a long time—the challenge can seem formidable. I messed it up myself until I received some great guidance.

I was one of the youngest members of my MBA class at Duke University's Fuqua School of Business. Because I had less work experience than most of my peers, I needed an excellent summer internship—not only to learn my way around the corporate world but also to set myself up better for full-time job opportunities.

A particular Fortune 500 company was coming onto campus to interview. I signed up and prepared the best way I knew: reading the company's annual report and industry news, thinking through some obvious questions, and making sure my new gray suit, white shirt, and red tie were ready. Yes, it was a cutting-edge look.

The recruiter and I met in a small conference room. He was a senior manager at the company (his gray suit was nicer than mine). The conversation went well until he asked a question I wasn't expecting: "Jim, if I spoke with some of your classmates later this afternoon how would they describe you?"

At that moment my brain apparently ceased working. I said something on the order of "Well, I'm sure they would say I'm a fun guy." I could tell the recruiter was no longer taking me seriously. It was an embarrassing moment, one I could not repeat.

After a bit of moping, I sought help from Dr. Bob Reinheimer, a faculty member and expert in management communications. When I asked his advice, he told me to take out a piece of paper and said, "I want you to draw out a table with five columns and three rows beneath. Let's start with the columns. They are for attributes you have, things about you."

I asked, "Dr. Bob, what should those things be?" He replied, "I don't know. You need to figure that part out. What are the things about you that help define you? Are you creative? Do you persevere? Do you have grit, ambition? Do you work well with others? Take some time. Then take your list to family members and friends, people who know you well and will be honest with you."

This started to make sense. "Okay, I understand what the columns are for. What about the rows underneath each column?"

He said, "The first of those is for examples, the ones that highlight the quality you want to convey. If one of your chosen attributes is creativity, you should have a couple of ninety-second stories that demonstrate that creativity. The stories could draw from your employment, but they don't have to. Remember that a good story is short, it describes the situation you confronted, it details what you did (to use that creativity), and it highlights the final net result of your efforts. What happened because of what you did? You should be able to find at least two examples under each of your attributes."

I asked, "What if I can't come up with two examples?"

"Then that should tell you something," Dr. Bob said. "It probably isn't a defining attribute."

He went on. "That last row is important. Use it to fill in vital information for the specific job at hand, and answer these questions: So what? Why is this ability relevant? How would you use it in the specific position for which you are interviewing? Many of your attributes and stories will stay consistent because they provide a depiction of you. But during your conversations with a potential employer, you'll still need to make the connection between the abilities you have and the things needed in the job."

You can probably tell where Dr. Bob was leading me. By taking the time to fill in ten cells in a table—and doing it seriously—I would produce ten authentic stories. Plus, I would be able to connect the dots between my personal attributes and how I would use them in a particular job. Equipped with those, I would be ready for nearly any interview situation in the future. After a few weeks I did get a great summer internship and, despite my relative inexperience, multiple job offers the following spring.

STORYTELLING TO BUILD IDENTITY

Personal stories can help you professionally, whether you are just starting out or have been around awhile. Just ask Chris Duke.

Chris was one of my classmates at Duke's Fuqua School of Business (but no, he is not part of *that* Duke family). He grew up in Kentucky, around lots of aunts, uncles, and cousins for whom cooking was part of the family tradition. During the 1930s, widowed and in need of extra money to support a family of nine children, Chris's grandmother Lourena began to make pies and cakes in her home for sale to local restaurants. Lourena passed those skills on to her nine children, including Chris's mother Anna Duke.

After a career that included sales for a pharmaceutical company, consulting for several global technology companies, and several years as a director for one of the companies surviving the dot-com boom and bust, Chris and his wife Debbie were ready for a change. They gathered traditional recipes, added a few twists, and started Anna's Gourmet Goodies (named for their daughter). After two years of organically growing the business on the side, they launched a full-time venture in 2003.

That is a neat story on its own. However, Chris came to recognize the larger power of storytelling itself to build the new family business. He and Debbie had begun with a model similar to his grandmother's—baking and selling wholesale desserts for restaurants. "Being in the wholesale business means you survive on volume," Chris says. "The idea of creating a personalized experience with customers was appealing." They began to experiment with gift boxes of cookies, which did not require refrigeration and could be packaged for a tailored customer experience. They did demos for local Realtors, participated in trade shows, and basically looked for areas of traction. "During that time one thing became clear," Chris explained. "People seemed to light up when I told the story of our business."

Chris launched a blog, *OutsideTheOven.com*, to share stories about the business, entrepreneurship, family, and giving. By 2017 he compiled many of these stories into a self-published book (*Outside the Oven: Observations on Life and Business from an Entrepreneur and Philosophical Baker)* because, as he wrote in the introduction, "I've always been interested in the backstory."

I can report to you firsthand that the cookies from Anna's Gourmet Goodies are quite good. But then again, there are lots of good cookies out there. As discussed in Chapter 4, the very structure of good stories serves our brains well. Even if you're a small player in a crowded industry with lots of marketplace noise, the right type of message will ensure you stand out.

"SOMEONE WHO'S DOING IT RIGHT": BIG SUCCESS WITH A ME-TOO PRODUCT

Many products and services, by their very nature, tend to go unnoticed. They don't lend themselves to conversation or prompt joy the way a chocolate chip cookie might. In those cases, the personal touch of your messengers might be the only way to move the growth needle. I once heard all about one of those unusually good messengers.

At the time, I was chief marketing officer for Mountain Valley Spring Company. One of our businesses was a seven-location HOD (Home and Office Delivery) company with operations stretching from Kansas City to Charleston, South Carolina. The work days were all about selling, scheduling, and delivering cases of bottled water, large bottles and coolers, coffee, and snacks. There were dozens and dozens of individual products available to customers. We competed against other delivery services but even more so against do-it-yourself.

From a marketer's perspective, the HOD world represents unusual opportunity on a daily basis. We were actually invited inside the homes and offices of our customers!

Each visit was a chance for conversation. Were we taking full advantage of those opportunities? I had only been on the job a short time, so I was visiting our various locations to learn the markets and speak directly with some of our customers.

One afternoon I was chatting with one such customer, the owner of a design firm. He reported that everything about our service was, from his standpoint, just fine. "Your guy does his job. From what I can tell he makes the deliveries, is in and out, pretty efficient. I can't remember his name but I haven't heard any complaints." I took note of his words and his relative lack of enthusiasm. It all seemed a bit perfunctory.

As I thanked him for his time and was about to leave, this customer suddenly became animated. "You know, Jim, if you want to see someone who's doing it right then you need to talk to Jackie. He's our Mat Man." (In the spirit of transparency, I only seem to recall that the name was Jackie but cannot be sure. I just remember him as the Mat Man. Ah, middle age.)

"Mats?" I asked. "Like floor mats?"

"Exactly," said our customer.

Commercial floor mats are, literally, a low-level item for most businesses to consider. We step on them and rarely give them a second thought. There must be something special happening with this floor-mat service for our customer to mention it, unprompted.

"There's nothing special about the mats, but Jackie is something else," he continued. "He called on us a couple of years ago, on a rainy day. He pointed out that for our office to make a good impression, visitors should have a place to wipe their feet and store a wet umbrella. It wasn't that expensive, and we could go month-to-month with the service."

I noticed that there were several mats around the office, each with the firm's logo. I asked about that part. "That came a few months later. Jackie said that we have a nice logo on the wall of our entry, and that most of his clients decide to add a logo to their mats—you know, for consistency."

And the customer continued. "Then a few months after that, Jackie said to me, 'You might not know this but we offer carpet cleaning—because we are already in your office regularly we can clean the spots that need it without you having to call.'"

Clearly, the Mat Man man (who might have been named Jackie) was an expert at managing not just a commoditized commercial service but also his message. He took note of his customer's world (such as a lot of visitor traffic and the logo the business proudly displayed), then proactively shared observations and recommendations. He lowered the risk for the customer by not asking for any long-term commitment. He let his customer know about services they weren't aware of. He knew the people in the office. He didn't come across as pushy—in fact, it was just the opposite; his customer was actually proud to tell me how he bought from Jackie!

By contrast our HOD driver was doing "fine," providing satisfactory service, doing nothing wrong. But what if he was having customer conversations like the Mat Man? What if most of the people around your organization—whether they are onsite with customers or in a different role—were having those types of conversations with their friends and in your community?

I would have offered the Mat Man a job, on the spot, to manage our customer experience and help coach our drivers across the network. But I suspect he would have politely turned me down anyway. He was probably too busy, and having too much fun, continuing to grow his own business.

As I have learned, when it comes to delivering a more effective growth message it isn't necessary to add or switch out the people in your organization anyway. But it does take a solid strategy, high-level intention, and consistency.

WHAT WILL BE YOUR NEXT MESSAGING MOVE?

All of the insights, advice, and admonitions in the world won't amount to a hill of beans for your growth plans unless you can apply them.

I included these real stories to demonstrate how professionals and organizations—of all shapes and sizes—have put these principles to use. There are many more I could share, but I suspect you get the point.

Some will hesitate. They might assume this requires cranking up some long, arduous process. Do you want to know what actually can be a tough process for spreading your ideas? When I was in academe and conducted research, the process for publishing a paper required rounds of often punctilious reviews. Then, if my research was accepted into a particular journal, I still might have to wait months for it to appear in the next available issue. Later, when I was a corporate marketer, our advertisements and other media messages had to make the rounds (including legal and various regulatory agencies) to make sure we weren't getting ourselves into trouble.

By contrast, equipping yourself and your team for everyday business conversations generally takes a few months or, for smaller organizations, perhaps a few weeks. The process tends to energize your internal audiences rather than frustrate them or wear them out. If you go through the end-of-chapter exercises, your organization will have the necessary building blocks.

Others might hesitate because they want their message to be "perfect." With all due apologies to Lexus and their "relentless pursuit of perfection" slogan, a quest for message perfection will stop genuine and needed progress in its tracks. Sure, you will want to have your facts straight. But the goal is to grow by getting in the game—making sure your business is part of conversations people are already having (or at least should be).

You might gain inspiration from the ancient Greek word *teleios,* which refers to a point of perfection of character. This idea of perfection doesn't mean someone or something is flawless (good thing), but rather that it has reached a level of maturity or completeness. Or, as people used to say in my small hometown of Swainsboro, Georgia, "You don't need to fiddle with it anymore."

Perhaps you prefer inspiration from a more current source. For years I have been a big fan of Monty Python, the British comedy troupe who built a huge following through its TV show *Monty Python's Flying Circus* as well as successful feature films. One of the founders, John Cleese, has continued to build fame and fortune post–Monty Python with the TV series *Fawlty Towers,* by writing and starring in movies, and even by producing management training videos for business.

On a Harvard Business Review IdeaCast podcast, Mr. Cleese was asked whether he is a perfectionist. He replied in part with this:

> *There are two ways you can be a perfectionist . . . one*
> *way is to try to make something as good as you can,*
> *which is what I do every night when I go on stage. The*
> *other side is the person who goes on agonizing about it.*

The professionals who are most effective in managing their message work to get their words, examples, and stories as good as they can make them. But they don't agonize, and they don't let the pursuit of some unattainably perfect message keep them from acting. That would lead to a continuing series of missed opportunities. Not even John Cleese could make that result funny.

The not-so-secret secret to business growth is usually right in front of us. Please don't wait for your message to be perfect, because it will never be. There is no better time to silence the crickets, lasso the cowboys, and refuse to be treated as a commodity.

Just imagine how many conversational opportunities will be waiting for you out there tomorrow.

BIBLIOGRAPHY

CHAPTER 1

Berger, Jonah (2013). *Contagious: Why Things Catch On*. New York: Simon & Schuster.

How Much Time Will the Average Person Spend on Social Media During Their Life? *www.adweek.com*

Cutting, James E., Kaitlin L. Brunick, Jordan E. DeLong, Catalina Iricinschi, and Ayse Candan (2011). "Quicker, faster, darker: Changes in Hollywood film over 75 years," *Iperception* 2(6), 569–576.

Millennials Engage with Their Smartphones More than They Do Actual Humans. *www.marketwatch.com*

The Football Playbook Rule? "Keeping It Simple" Is the Way to Go. *www.pressherald.com*

CHAPTER 2

Goodwin, Kimberly, Bennie Waller, and H. Shelton Weeks (2014). "The Impact of Broker Vernacular in Residential Real Estate," *Journal of Housing Research* 23(2), 143–161.

The Advertising Archives. *www.advertisingarchives.co.uk*

The John W. Hartman Center for Sales, Advertising, and Marketing History. *https://library.duke.edu*

We Analyzed 752,626 Facebook Ads, and Here's What We Learned (2018 Update). *https://adespresso.com*

New Study Shows Which Words Sell, and Which Don't. *www .seattletimes.com*

Berger, Christopher and H. Henrik Ehrsson (2013). "Mental Imagery Changes Multisensory Perception," *Current Biology*, published online June 27, 2013 at *www.cell.com*

How Much Longer Will Consumers Keep Buying Cars at Dealerships? *www.digitaltrends.com*

Abrahams, Jeffrey (1999). *The Mission Statement Book: 301 Corporate Mission Statements from America's Top Companies*. Berkeley, CA: Ten Speed Press.

"Mission Statement" Words. *www.forbes.com*

The Ideal Length of a Sales Email, Based on 40 Million Emails. *https://blog.hubspot.com*

The Industries Where People Stay in Their Jobs the Longest. *www.forbes.com*

Newman, Adam Andrew (November 27, 2008). "Why Time Stands Still for Watchmakers," *The New York Times*, *www.nytimes.com*

A Short History of the Rise, Fall and Rise of Subliminal Messaging. *www.scientificamerican.com*

Domino's Tracking App Tells You Who Made Your Pizza—Or Does It? *www.wsj.com*

Kovacs, Balazs, Glenn R. Carroll, and David W. Lehman (2014). "Authenticity and Consumer Value Ratings: Empirical Tests from the Restaurant Domain," *Organization Science*, 25(2), 458–478.

Closing the Loop on Charlotte's Cookie Caper. *http://mikerowe.com*

CHAPTER 3

A number of great Lou Holtz quotes are included in a news story from Dick Harmon: "Lou Holtz, ESPN part ways but his quotes, personality will endure," *Deseret News*, April 13, 2015. See *www.deseretnews.com*

Frank Newport's summary of Americans' perceived time crunch over the years. *https://news.gallup.com*

Linda Stone's summary and research on Continuous Partial Attention. *https://lindastone.net*

Galinsky, Adam D., Joe C. Magee, M. Ena Inesi, and Deborah H. Gruenfeld (2006). "Power and Perspectives Not Taken," *Psychological Science* 17(12), 1068–1074.

Adrian Ward's review of the neuroscience of talking about ourselves. *www.scientificamerican.com*

Tamir, Diana I. and Jason P. Mitchell (2012). "Disclosing Information About the Self Is Intrinsically Rewarding," *Proceedings of the National Academy of Sciences* 109 (21), 8038–8043.

The Edelman Trust Barometer: *www.edelman.com*

Edelman surveyed Americans about trust. The findings are disturbing, but not in the way you might think. *www.washingtonpost.com*

Kahneman, Daniel (2011). *Thinking, Fast and Slow*. New York: Farrar, Straus, and Giroux.

Toman, Nicholas, Brent Adamson, and Cristina Gomez (2017). "The New Sales Imperative," *Harvard Business Review* March–April, 118–125.

CHAPTER 4

Why Don't Buyers Want to Meet With Your Salespeople? *https://go.forrester.com*

Zak, Paul J. (2017). "The Neuroscience of Trust," *Harvard Business Review*, January–February, 84–90.

Quieting the Lizard Brain. *https://seths.blog*

Wammes, Jeffrey D., Melissa E. Meade, and Myra A. Fernandes (2016). "The Drawing Effect: Evidence for Reliable and Robust Memory Effects in Free Recall," *Quarterly Journal of Experimental Psychology* 69(9), 1752–1776.

Mueller, Pam A. and Daniel M. Oppenheimer (2014). "The Pen Is Mightier than the Keyboard: Advantages of Longhand Over Laptop Note Taking," *Psychological Science* 25(6), 1159–1168.

3 Ways to Spot a Bad Statistic. *www.ted.com*

Fifty-nine Percent of Consumers Around the World Indicate Difficulty Understanding Nutritional Labels. *www.nielsen.com*

Mark Levy. *www.levyinnovation.com*

CHAPTER 5

Pink, Daniel H. (2012). *To Sell Is Human: The Surprising Truth about Moving Others.* New York: Riverhead Books.

Statistics on sales and related occupation: *www.bls.gov*

Honesty/Ethics in Professions. *www.gallup.com*

Sirianni, Nancy J., Mary Jo Bitner, Stephen W. Brown, and Naomi Mandel (2013). "Branded Service Encounters: Strategically Aligning Employee Behavior with the Brand Positioning," *Journal of Marketing* 77 (November), 108–123.

Barrick, Murray R., M. K. Mount, and T. A. Judge (2001), "Personality and Performance at the Beginning of the New Millennium: What Do We Know and Where Do We Go Next?" *International Journal of Selection and Assessment,* 9, 9–30.

Grant, Adam M. (2013). "Rethinking the Extraverted Sales Ideal: The Ambivert Advantage," *Psychological Science* 24(6), 1024–1030.

de Boer, Ruud, Paul Schermerhorn, Jan Gademan, Gert de Groot, and Gerrit Jan van Ingen Schenau (1986). "Characteristic Stroke Mechanics of Elite and Trained Male Speed Skaters," *Journal of Applied Biomechanics* 2(3), 175–185.

de Pascalis, Vilredo (2004). "On the Psychophysiology of Extraversion," in *On the Psychobiology of Personality: Essays in Honor of Marvin Zuckerman,* edited by Robert M. Stelmack. Boston: Elsevier.

Facebook by the Numbers: Stats, Demographics & Fun Facts. *www.omnicoreagency.com*

Goldfarb, Avi, Ryan McDevitt, Sampsa Samila, and Brian Silverman (2015). "The Effect of Social Interaction on Economic Transactions: Evidence from Changes in Two Retail Formats," *Management Science* 61(12), 2963–2981.

The Beloit College Mindset List: Class of 2021: *www.beloit.edu*

CHAPTER 6

The Town Crier. *www.historic-uk.com*

Top Town Crier to Be Crowned as Hebden Bridge Hits 500. *http:// news.bbc.co.uk*

World's Most Admired Companies. *http://fortune.com*

You Won't Believe How Nike Lost Steph to Under Armour. *www .espn.com*

Michael Jordan's Net Worth Jumps $350 Million to $1.65 Billion. *www.forbes.com*

Morgan Stanley: Stephen Curry Could Be Worth $14 Billion to Under Armour. *www.businessinsider.com*

Bruce Braley Posts Photo of English Farm, Takes It Down. *www .buzzfeednews.com*

PBS Admits Using Old Fireworks Footage in Fourth of July Broadcast. *www.nytimes.com*

It's Our Fault! American's Ads Say "Great Flyers" Know How to Handle the Hassles of Air Travel. *www.forbes.com*

Changing Minds and Changing Towels. *https://www .psychologytoday.com*

Drake University's Ad Campaign Gets Big D+. *www.adweek.com*

Dove: Campaign for Real Beauty. *http://adage.com*

Dove Ad Underscores Tense Cultural Moment for Advertisers. *www.usatoday.com*

Unilever Apologizes for Dove Ad. *www.wsj.com*

Ferris Bueller's Day Off. Dir. John Hughes. Perf. Matthew Broderick, Alan Ruck, and Mia Sara. Paramount Pictures, 1999.

10 Tips for Dealing with Crisis Communication. *http://plankcenter .ua.edu*

CHAPTER 7

Millennials Are the Largest Generation in the U.S. Labor Force. *www.pewresearch.org*

Liu, Wei, Gert Pasman, Jenneke Taal-Fokker, and Pieter Jan Stappers (2014). "Exploring Generation Y Interaction Qualities at Home and at Work," *Cognition, Technology, and Work* 16, 405–415.

Hartman, Jackie L. and Jim McCambridge (2011). "Optimizing Millennials' Communication Styles," *Business Communication Quarterly* 74(1), 22–44.

Millennial Branding and Randstad US Release First Worldwide Study Comparing Gen Y and Gen Z Workplace Expectations. *https://www.prnewswire.com*

Goldfayn, Alex L. (2015). *The Revenue Growth Habit: The Simple Art of Growing Your Business by 15% in 15 Minutes a Day*. Hoboken, NJ: Wiley.

The Daily Mail reports on the effects of speaking with High Rising Terminal. Want a Promotion? Don't Speak Like an Aussie: Rising in Pitch at the End of Sentences Make You Sound "Insecure." *www.dailymail.co.uk*

Linneman, Thomas J. (2013). "Gender in Jeopardy! Intonation Variation on a Television Game Show," *Gender & Society* 27(1), 82–105.

Singh Ospina, N., K. A. Phillips, R. Rodriguez-Gutierrez, A. Castaneda-Guarderas, M. R. Gionfriddo, M. E. Branda, and V. M. Montori (2018). "Eliciting the Patient's Agenda—Secondary Analysis of Recorded Clinical Encounters," *Journal of General Internal Medicine* 34(1), 36–40.

Ubel, Peter, W. G. Unter, C. Z. Zhang, A. Hesson, J. K. Davis, C. Kirby, L. D. Williamson, and J. A. Barnett (2016). "What Strategies Do Physicians and Patients Discuss to Reduce Out-of-Pocket Costs? Analysis of Cost-Saving Strategies in 1755 Outpatient Clinic Visits," *Medical Decision Making* 36(7).

Machida, Moe, Rose Marie Ward, and Robin S. Vealey (2012). "Predictors of Sources of Self-Confidence in Collegiate Athletes," *International Journal of Sport and Exercise Psychology* 10(3), 172–185.

Gallup Poll on the Environment. *https://news.gallup.com*

For Earth Day, Here's How Americans View Environmental Issues. *www.pewresearch.org*

CHAPTER 8

Michael Porter and Nitin Nohria's study on How CEOs Manage Time. *https://hbr.org*

Cracking the Code of Change. *https://hbr.org*

The Key to Change Is Middle Management. *https://hbr.org*

From the Greater Good magazine: How Grateful Are Americans? *https://greatergood.berkeley.edu*

Grant, Adam M. and Francesca Gino (2010). "A Little Thanks Goes a Long Way: Explaining Why Gratitude Expressions Motivate Prosocial Behavior," *Journal of Personality and Social Psychology* 98(6), 946–955.

Lyubomirsky, Sonja and Kristin Layous (2013). "How Do Simple Positive Activities Increase Well-Being?" *Current Directions in Psychological Science* 22(1), 57–62.

A Social Psychologist Explains Why We Should Ask for Help More Often. *www.theverge.com*

CHAPTER 9

Prof. Benham Tabrizi: The Key to Change Is Middle Management. *https://hbr.org*

Gartner: Managers Can't Be Great Coaches All By Themselves. *www.gartner.com*

Charting the Differences Between Pedagogy and Andragogy. *www.educatorstechnology.com*

A Simple, Easy to Understand Guide to Andragogy. *www.cornerstone.edu*

Millennials Want to Be Coached at Work. *https://hbr.org*

Kotter, John P. (1990). *Leading Change.* Cambridge, MA: Harvard Business Review Press.

CHAPTER 10

Family businesses fight long odds to become legacies. *https://money.cnn.com*

Family Business Alliance: Cited Stats. *www.fbagr.org*

ATA International. *www.ataonline.com*

Arkansas Mutual Insurance Company. *www.arkansasmutual.com*

Alex Laskey's TEDx talk video: How Behavioral Science Can Lower Your Energy Bill. *www.youtube.com*

DSG Consulting's Opower case study: New Hire Onboarding and Scaling for Growth. *www.dsgconsulting.com*

The Feathered Head. *www.thefeatheredhead.com*

Chip Massey. *www.chipmassey.com*

Anna's Gourmet Goodies. *www.annasgourmetgoodies.com*

HBR IdeaCast interview with John Cleese: *https://soundcloud.com*

INDEX

ABOUT THE AUTHOR

JIM KARRH, PhD, helps business professionals, teams, and entire organizations lead more effective customer conversations—which in turn produces better customer relationships, stronger brands, and more growth opportunities. Jim leads his own consulting firm, Karrh & Associates (*www.JimKarrh.com*); he also serves as a consulting principal with DSG Consulting, one of the world's leading sales-enablement firms.

Whether clients need guidance in the form of consulting, speaking, or coaching, Jim can offer a valuable perspective rooted in both expertise and practical experience. He has served such clients as associations, small businesses, high-growth tech firms, North America's largest martial arts organization, and many members of the Fortune 500. As a corporate marketing leader, he helped America's oldest continuously produced brand of bottled water to grow again—building an integrated marketing and public relations program judged best in its industry by the International Bottled Water Association.

He is a popular speaker at industry events, including the CMO Summit, Packaging That Sells, UB Tech, and the Professional Convention Management Association as well as for corporate events such as the Jim Beam Global Economic Summit and Euronet USA.

Jim is host of the "Manage Your Message" podcast and a frequent guest on other leading podcasts. He is a regular contributor to the American Marketing Association Executive Circle blog, an award-winning columnist for Arkansas Business, and a guest contributor to many business and trade publications.

A recognized expert in marketing communications and buyer behavior, Jim has also served on the faculty of three universities. His research has been published in top peer-reviewed journals such as the *Journal of Advertising Research, Journal of Advertising, Journal of Applied Social Psychology*, and *Journal of Marketing for Higher Education*.

Jim earned his MBA from Duke University's Fuqua School of Business, where he was named a Fuqua Scholar and elected by his classmates to be class speaker at graduation. He earned PhD, MA, and BS degrees from the University of Florida.

Jim, his wife Alison, and their four children live in Little Rock, Arkansas. But their dogs run the house.